Fun Cacti Coloring Book

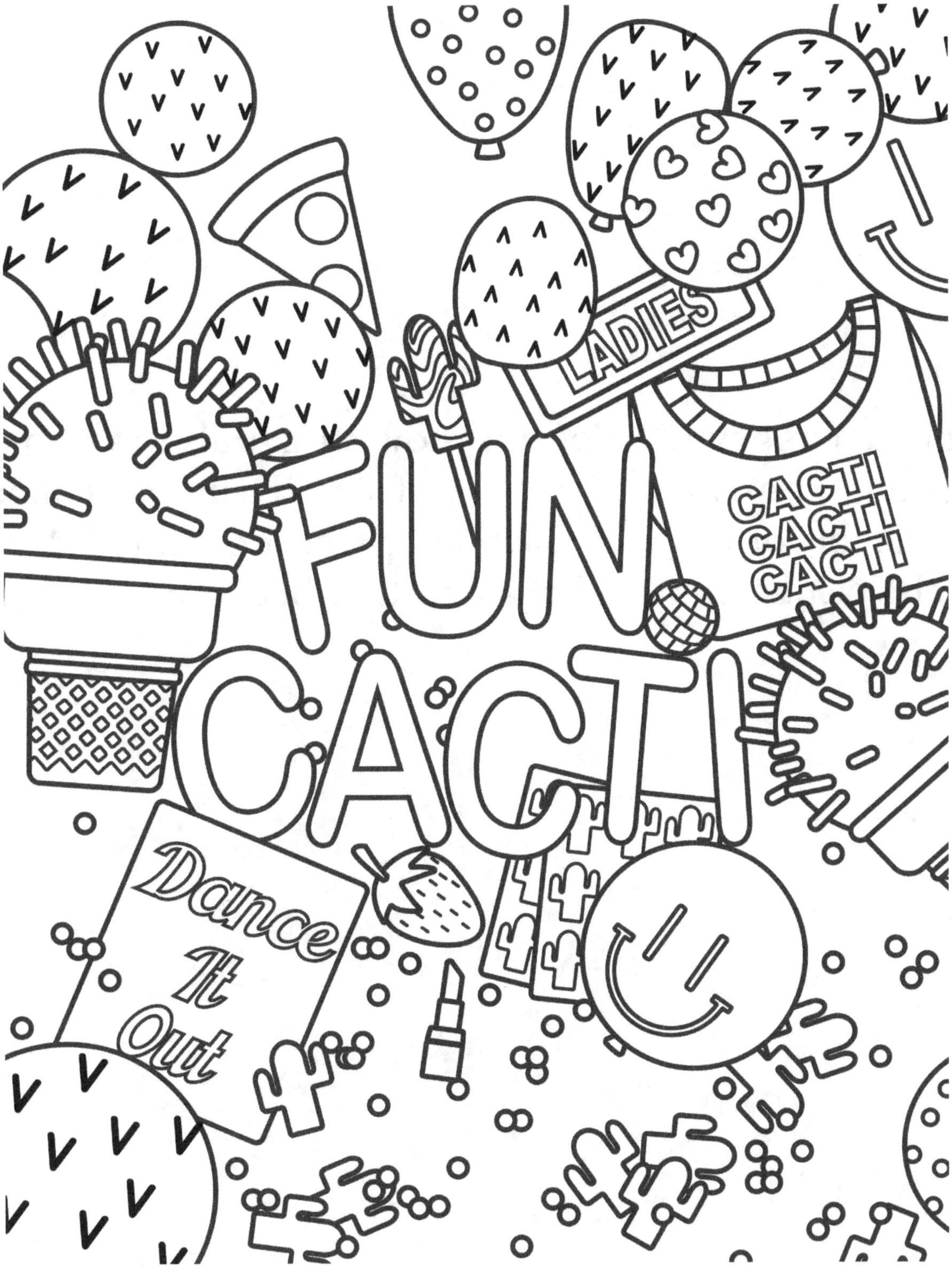

FUN CACTI

LADIES

CACTI CACTI CACTI

Dance It Out

Carolyn Coloring

Hey!

Let's Start The Relaxing!

Cuctus Flower Language

Erernal Love, Loneliess, Warmth and Enthusiasm

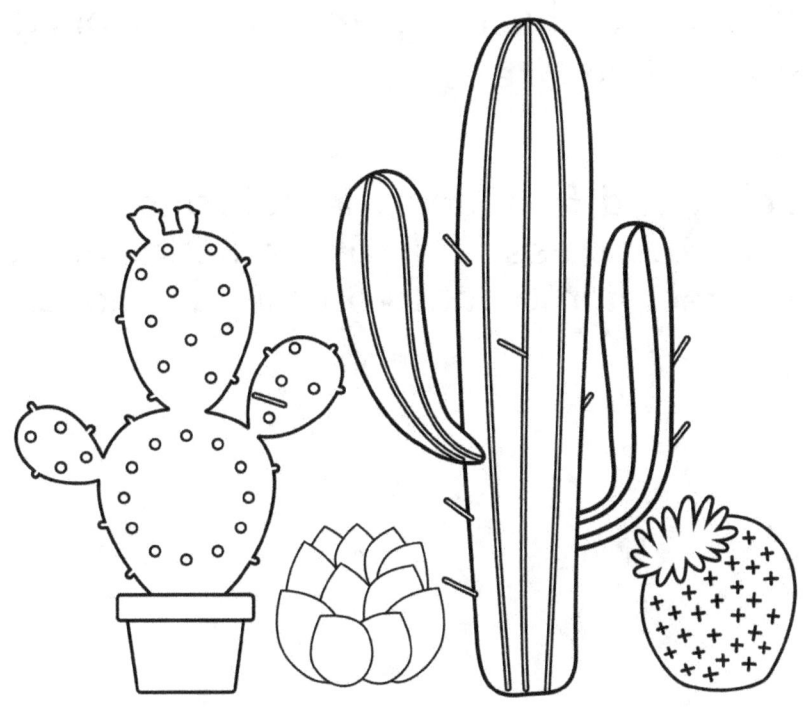

Enjoy!

his book includes a **Free Digital Copy** (PDF form
end of this paperback version. It's an awesome
you that you could print your favorite images
and color them an unlimited number of times.

:t your picture. Which image speaks to you today? 1
1e you should color.

se your palette. Select the colors you will be using f

.

1 coloring. This is the fun part. Don't worry about g
thing perfect, just start.

irself to relax and focus on the coloring. You'll find it i
vay to alleviate stress and take a little time out from
ssles. If you feel don't want to do it anymore, just stop

Color Charts Test

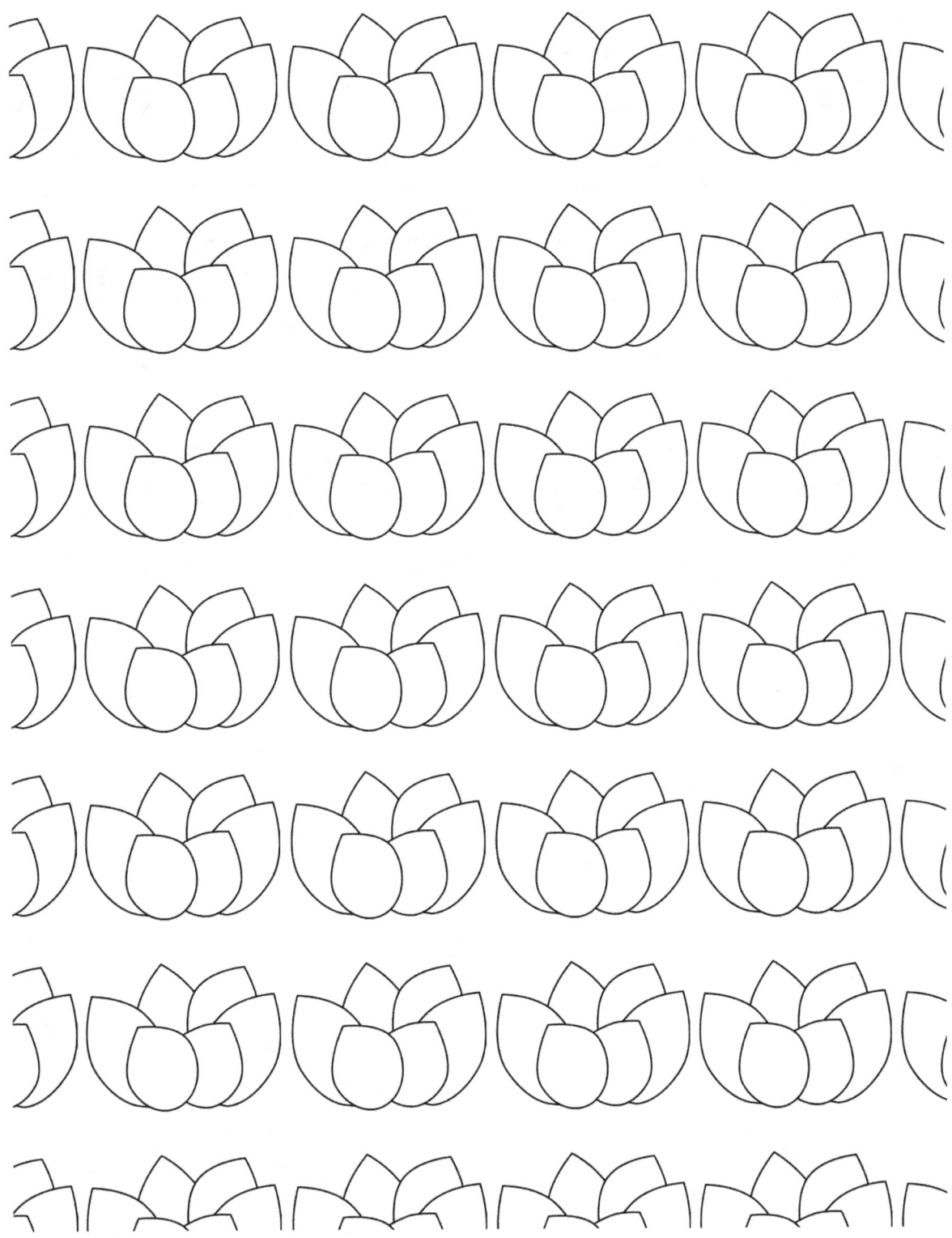

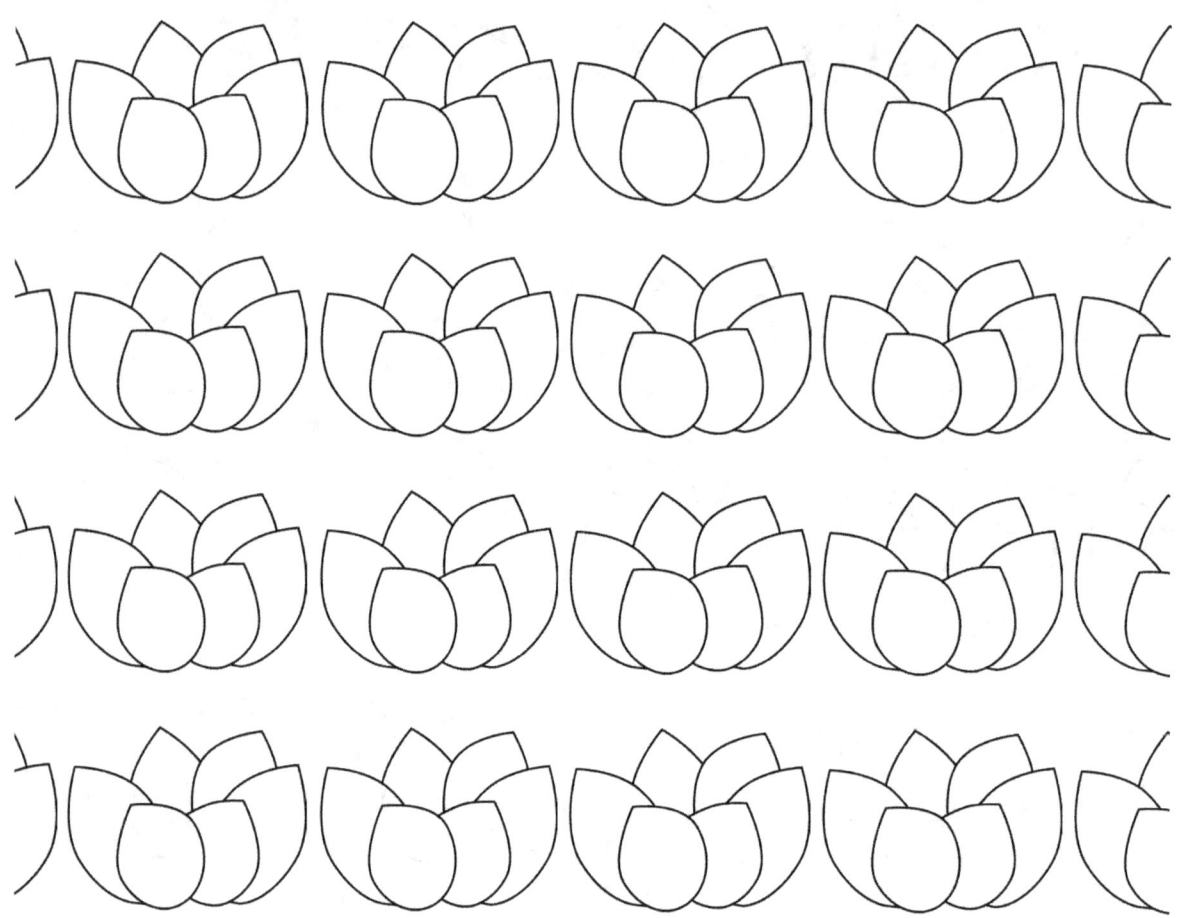

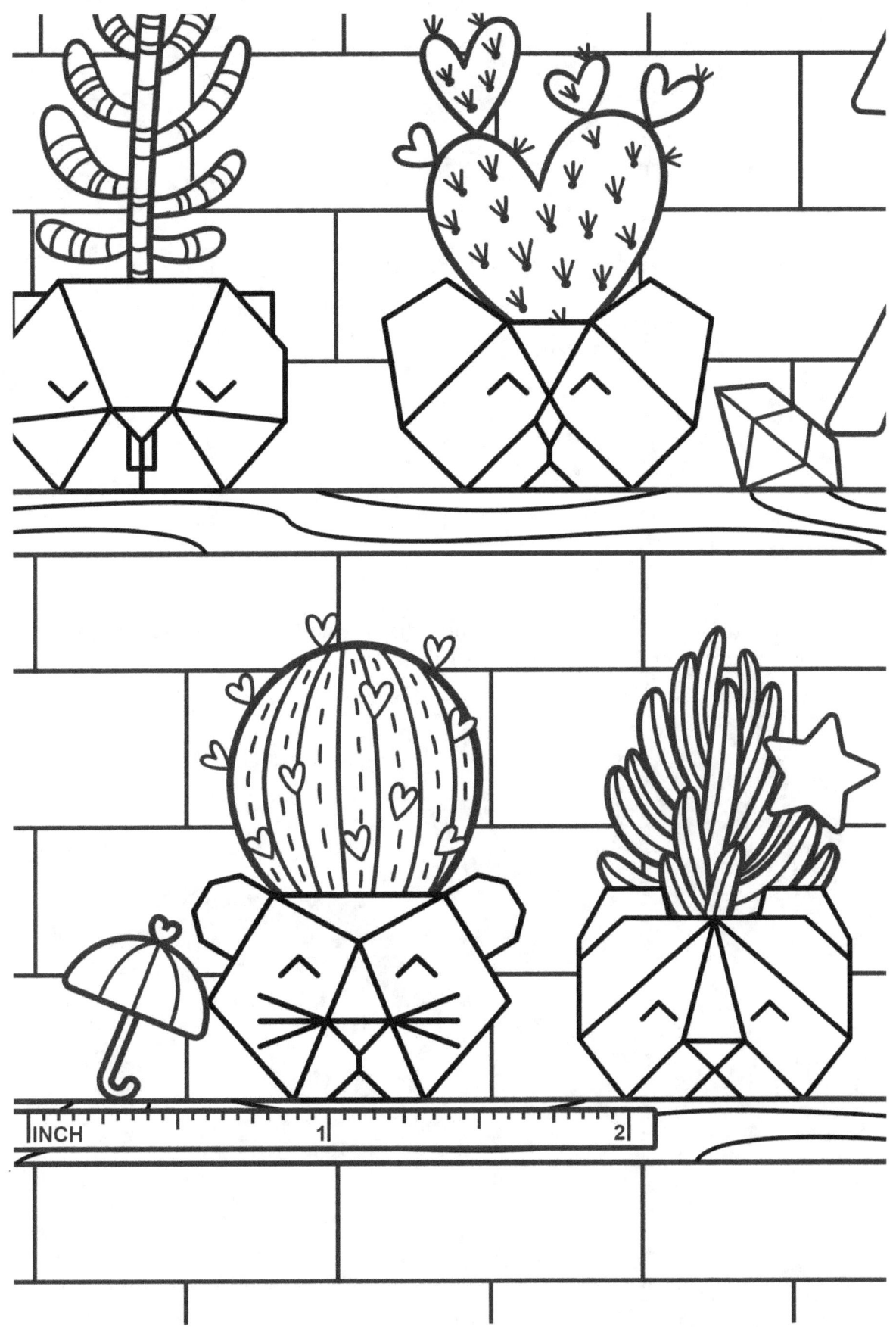

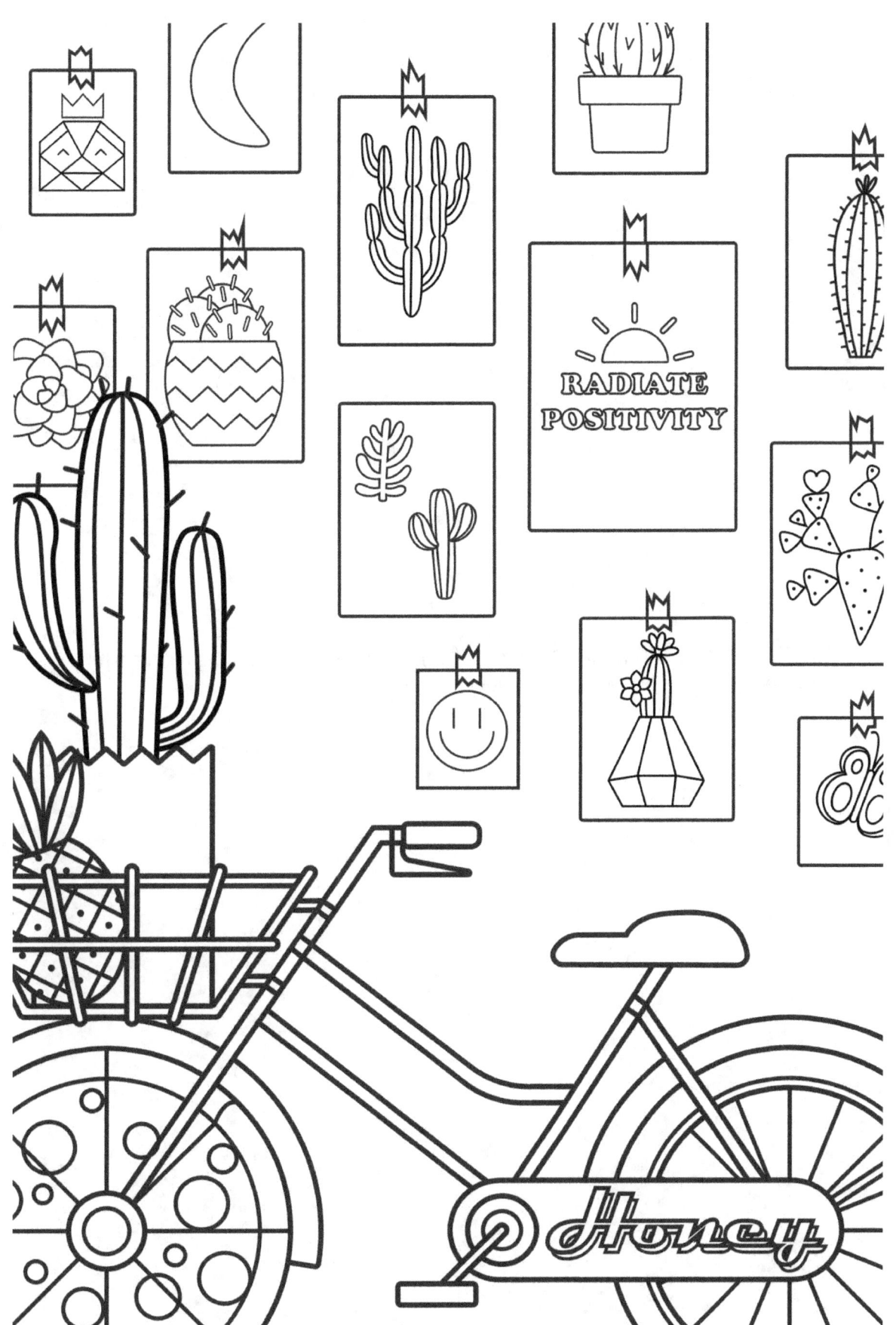

This is a Bleed Through Page. Find other great Titles by Searching for Mike Murphy on Your Favorite Book Retailer.

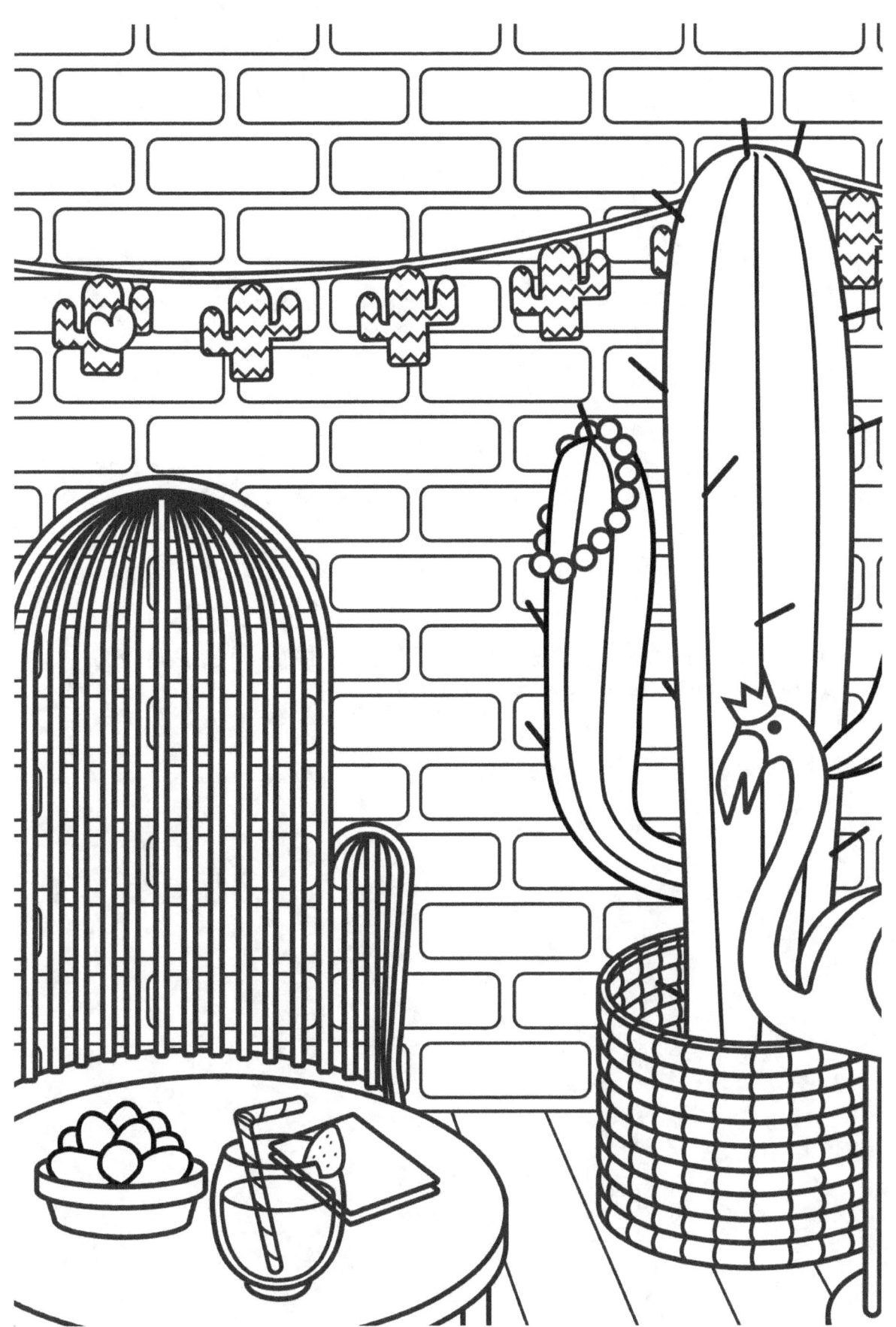

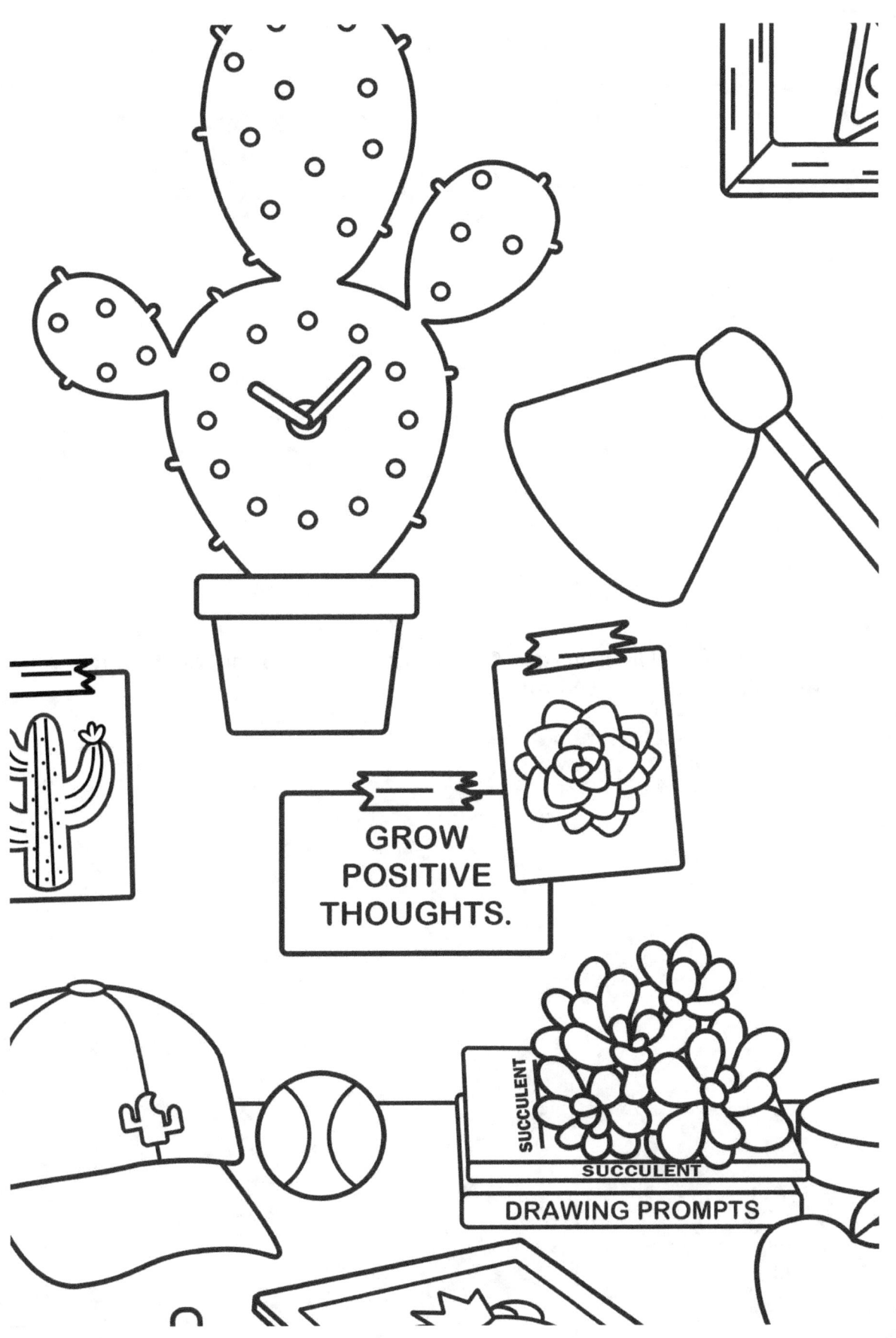

GROW
POSITIVE
THOUGHTS.

SUCCULENT

SUCCULENT

DRAWING PROMPTS

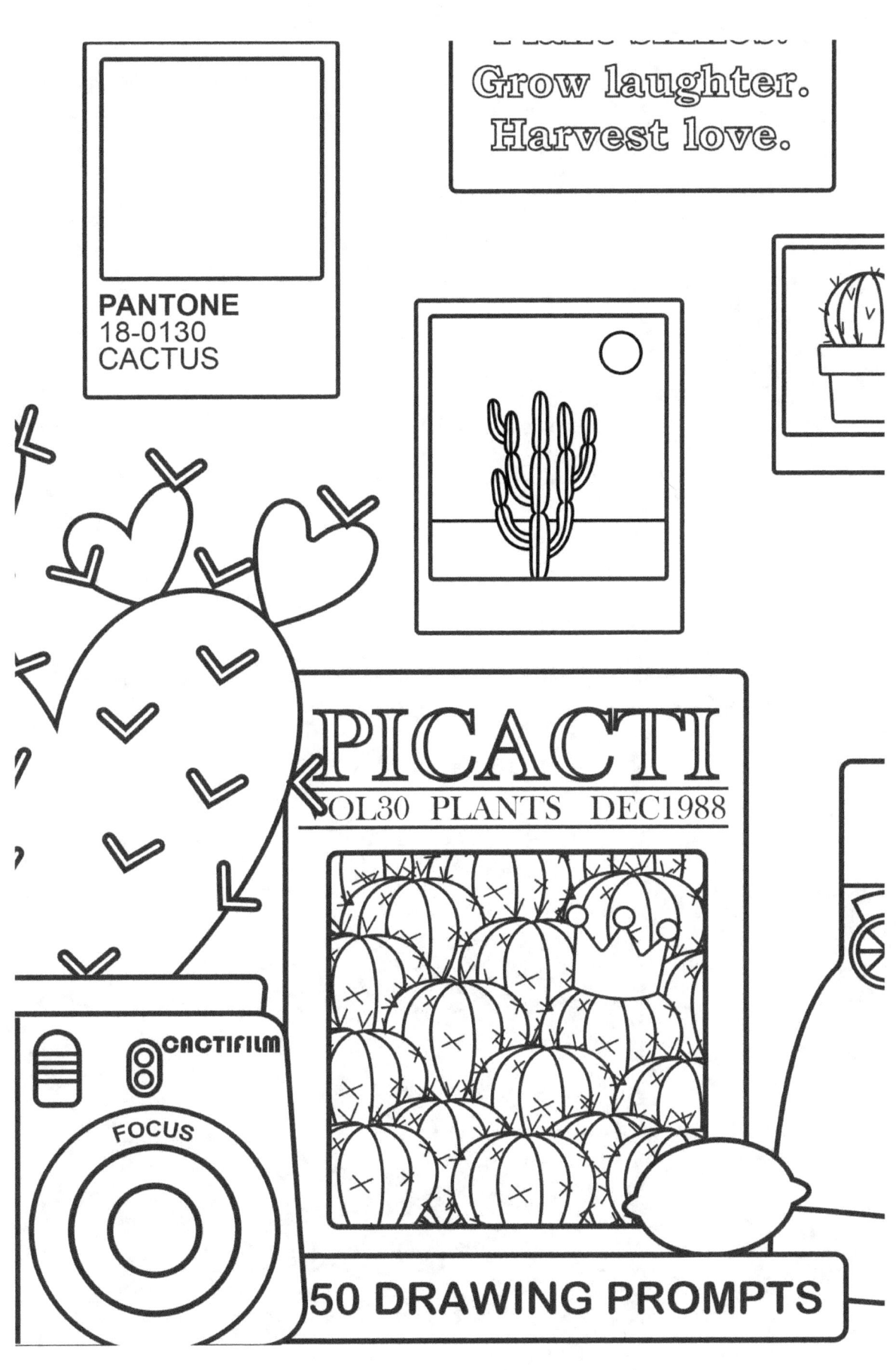

This is a Bleed Through Page. Find other great Titles by Searching for Mike Murphy on Your Favorite Book Retailer.

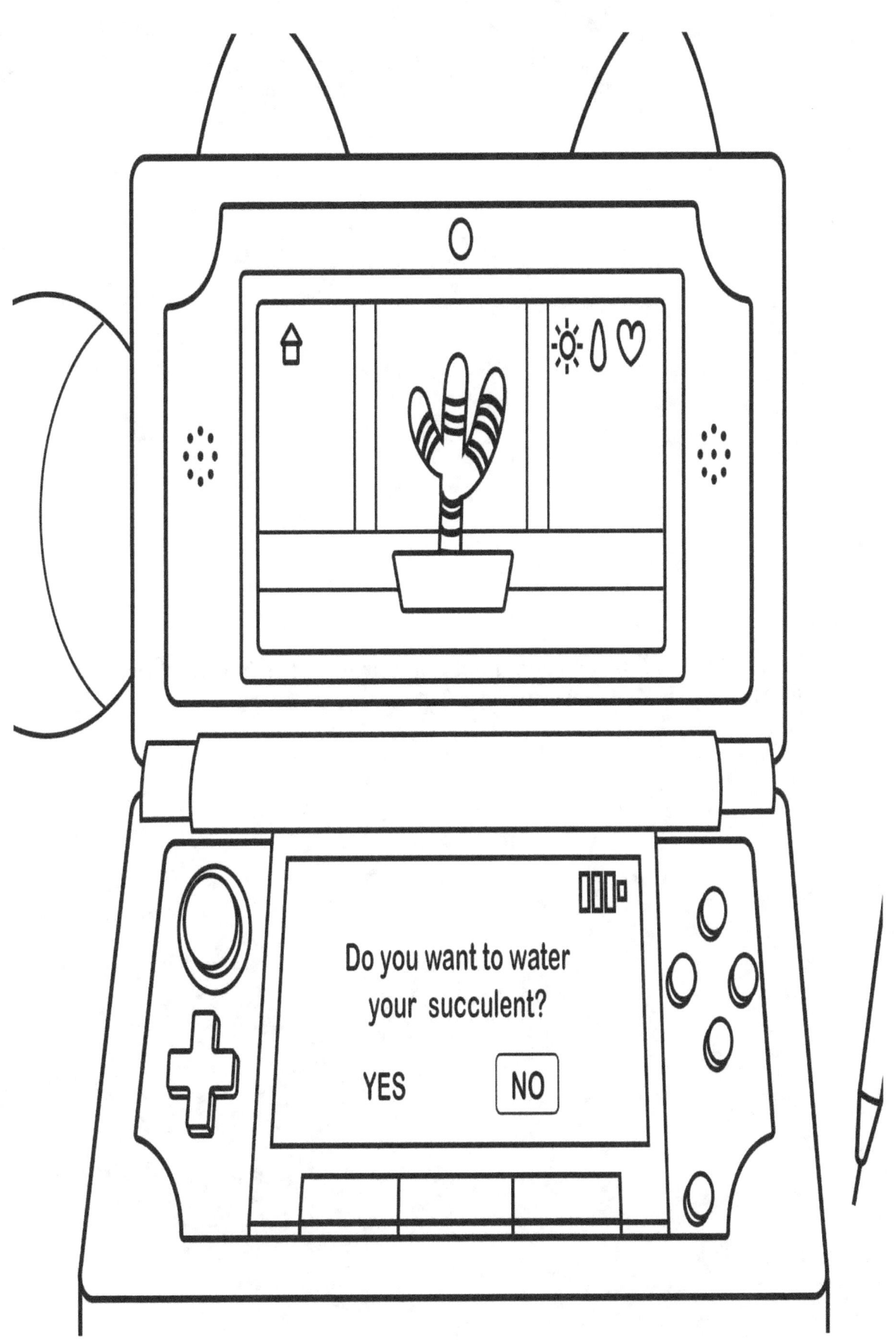

Do you want to water
your succulent?

YES NO

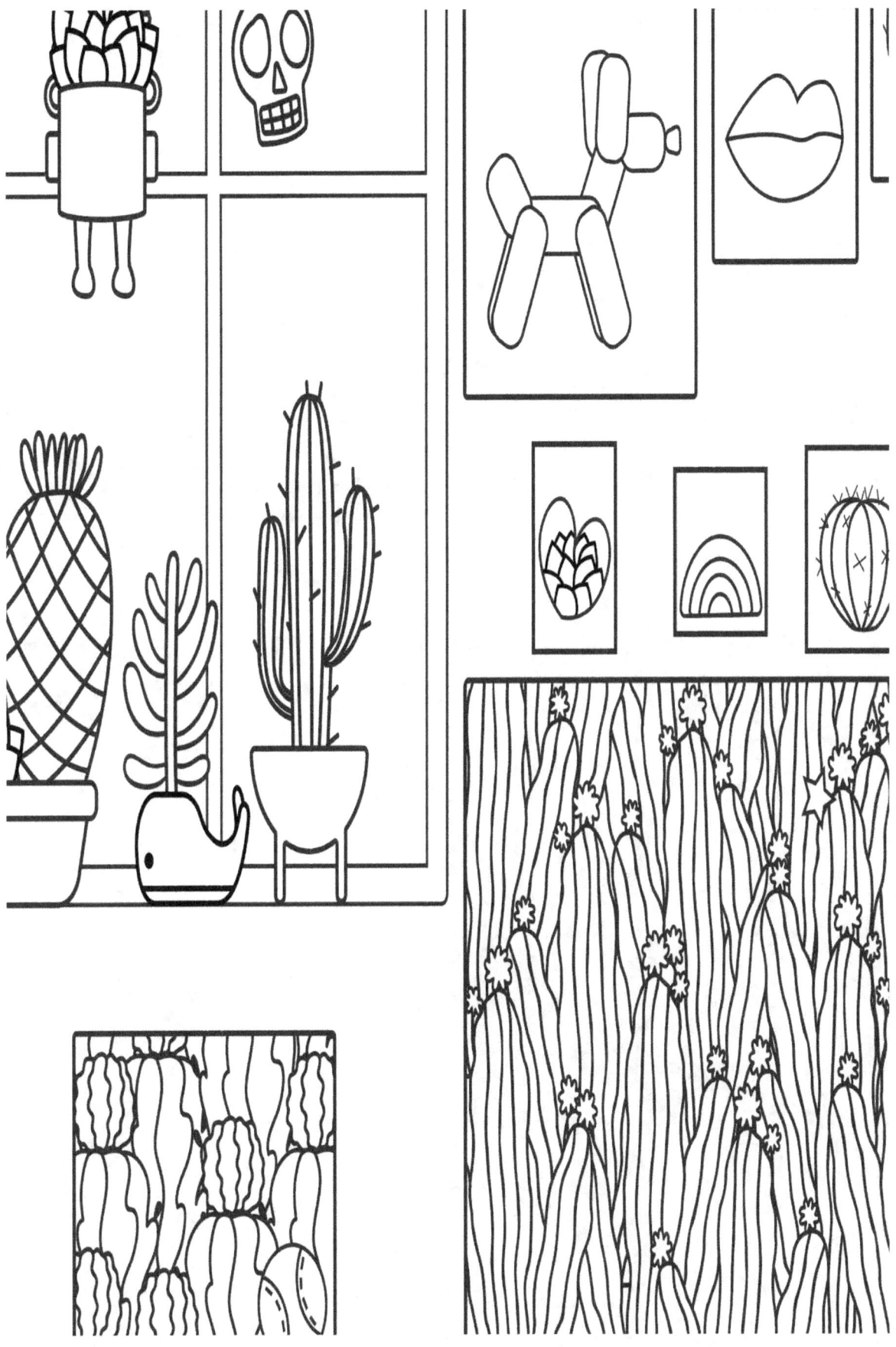

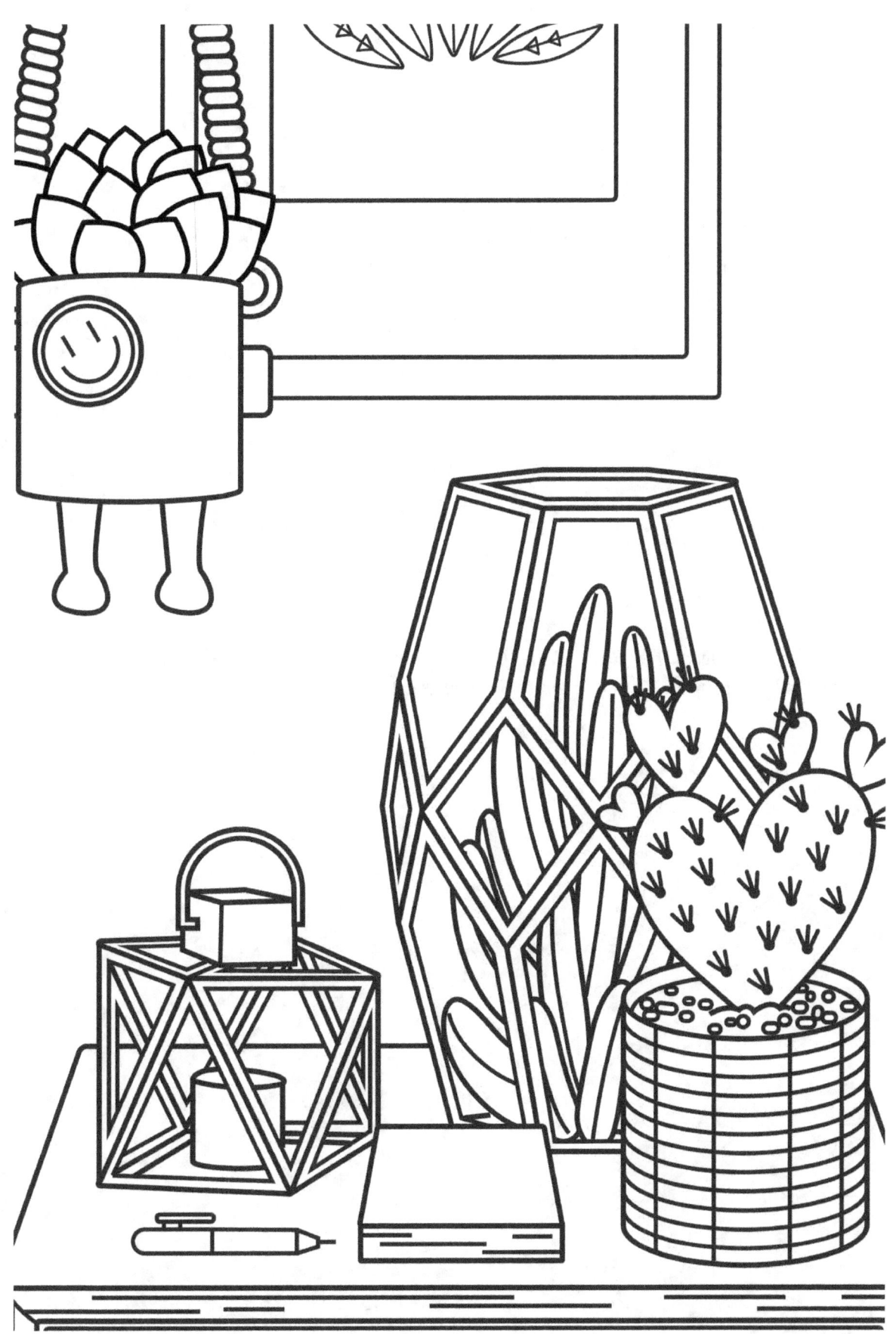

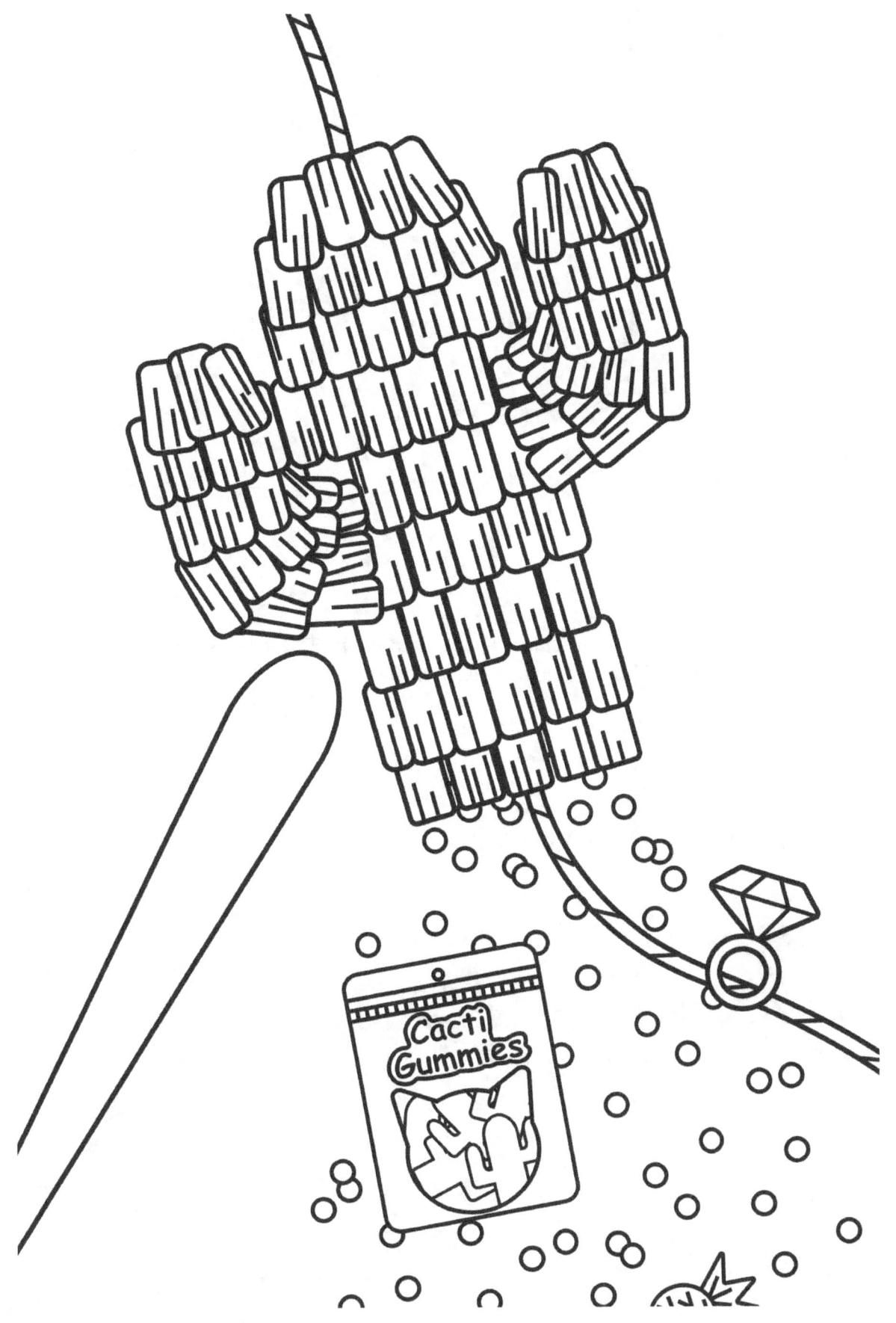

This is a Bleed Through Page. Find other great Titles by Searching for Mike Murphy on Your Favorite Book Retailer.

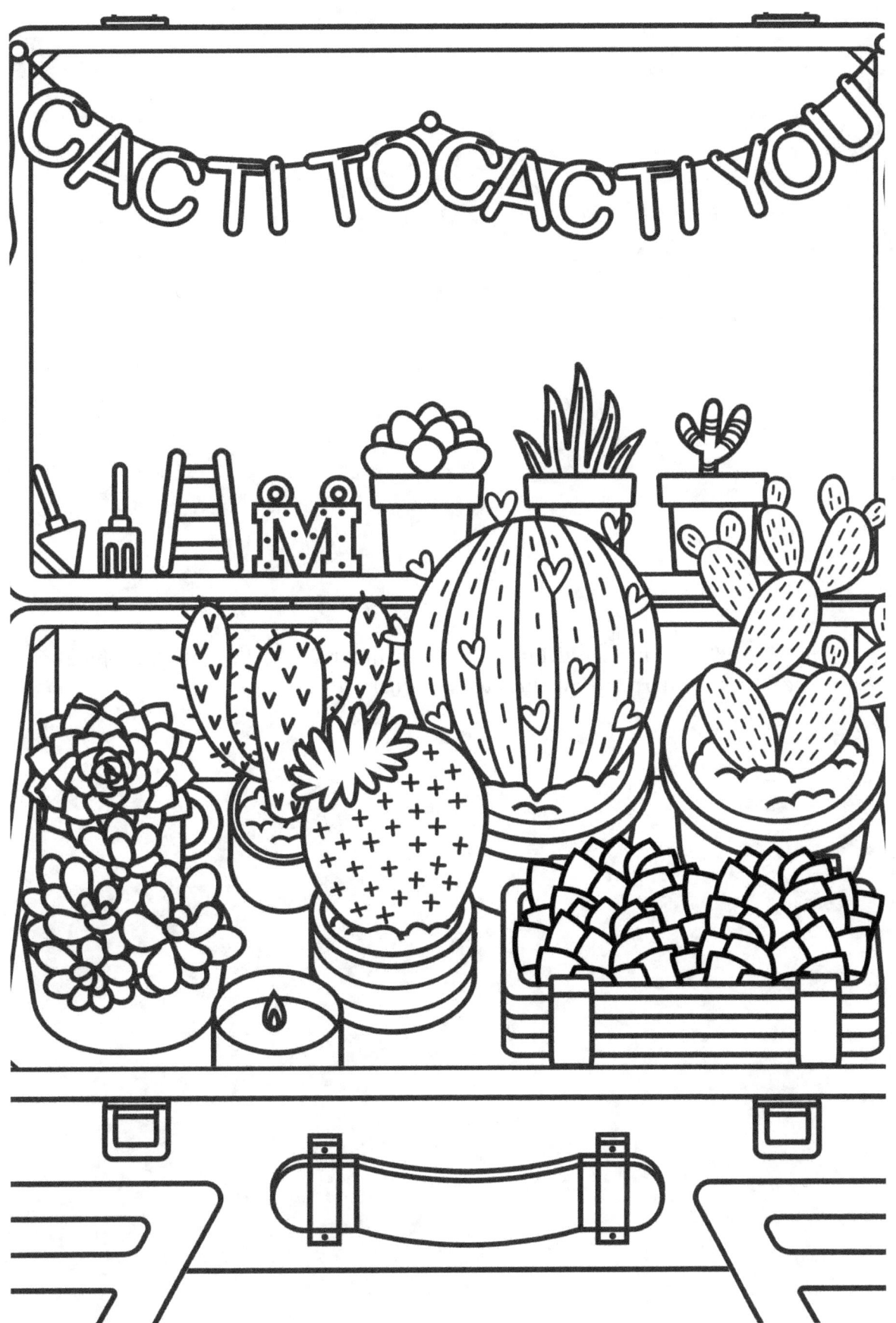

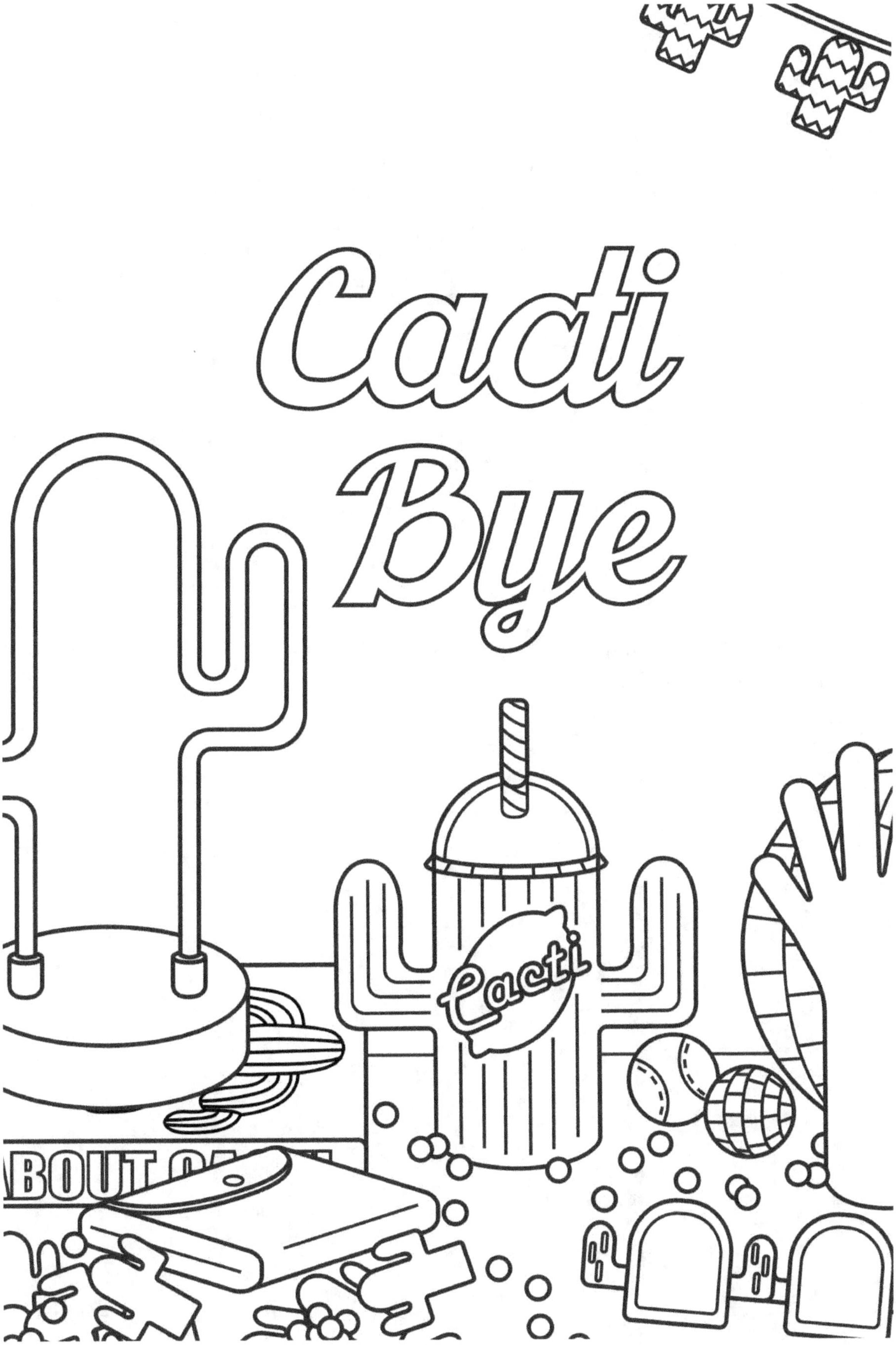

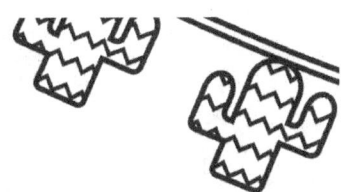

Cacti
Bye

Cacti

BOUT

This is a Bleed Through Page. Find other great Titles by Searching for Mike Murphy on Your Favorite Book Retailer.

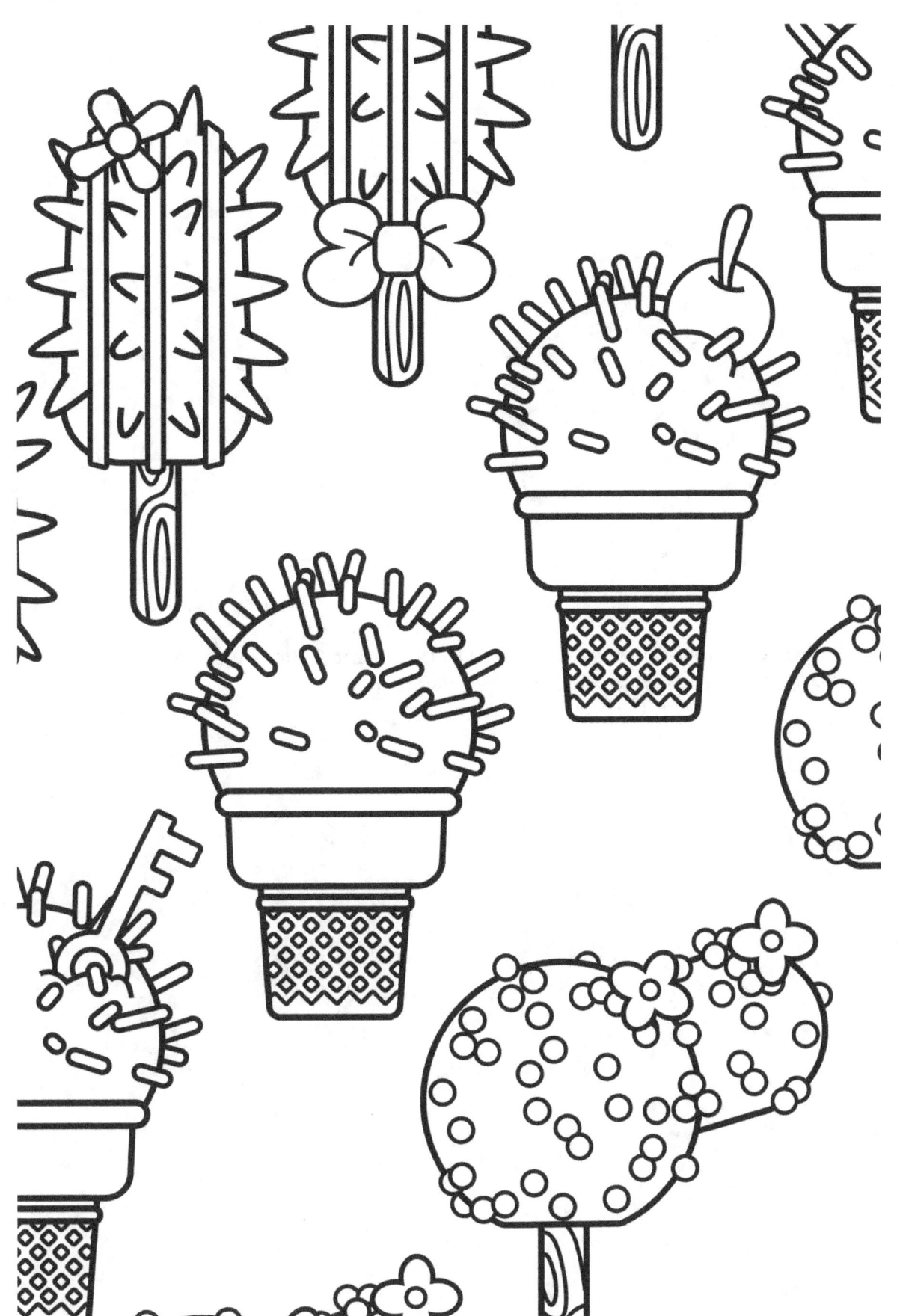

Succulent Treasures
Cacti Box
How to care for Cactus Garden

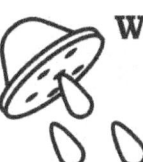
Water
Summer: Once a week
Winter: Once a month
Put the water in the soil,
not directly on the plant.

Soil
Use Good quality potting soil and
and change it every year. Also make
sure that has an appropriate drainage.
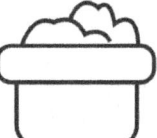

Sun
4 to 5 hours of direct
sunlight a day.

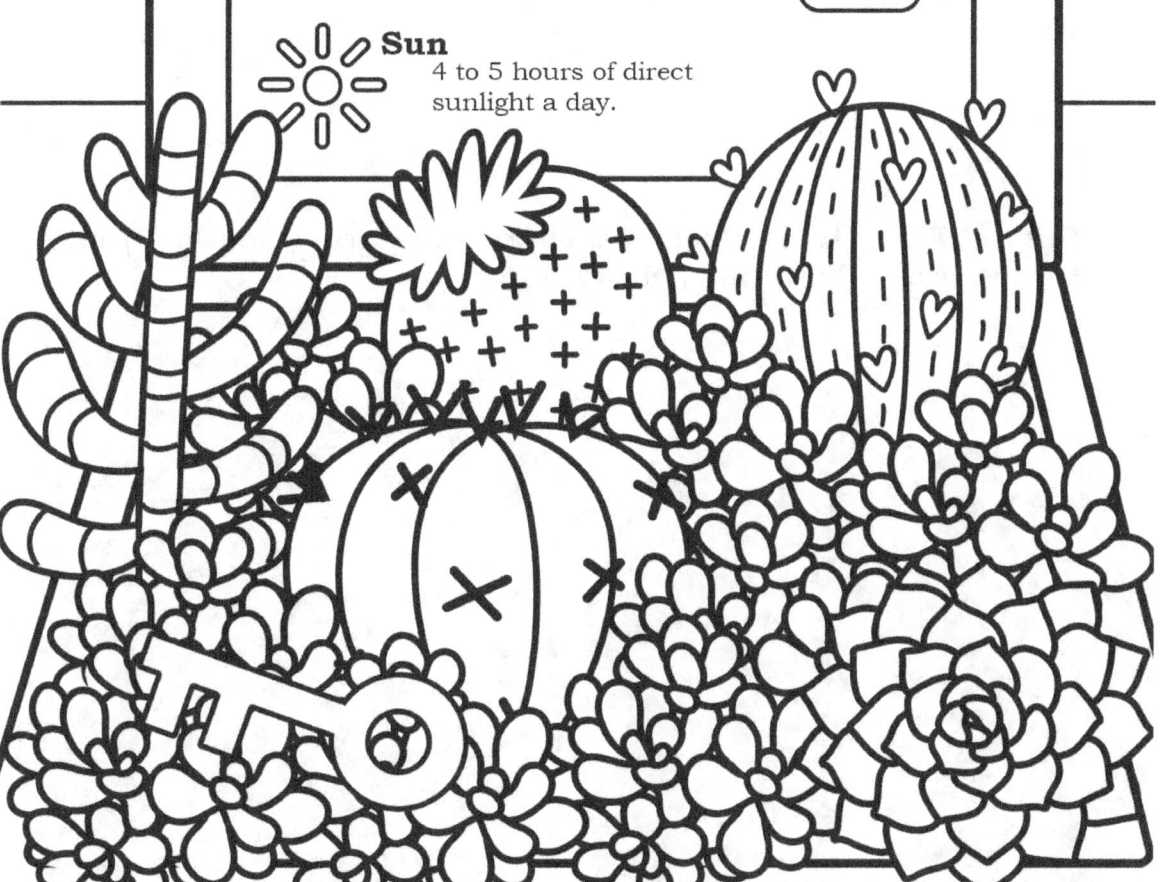

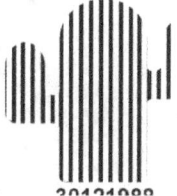

30131988

This is a Bleed Through Page. Find other great Titles by Searching for Mike Murphy on Your Favorite Book Retailer.

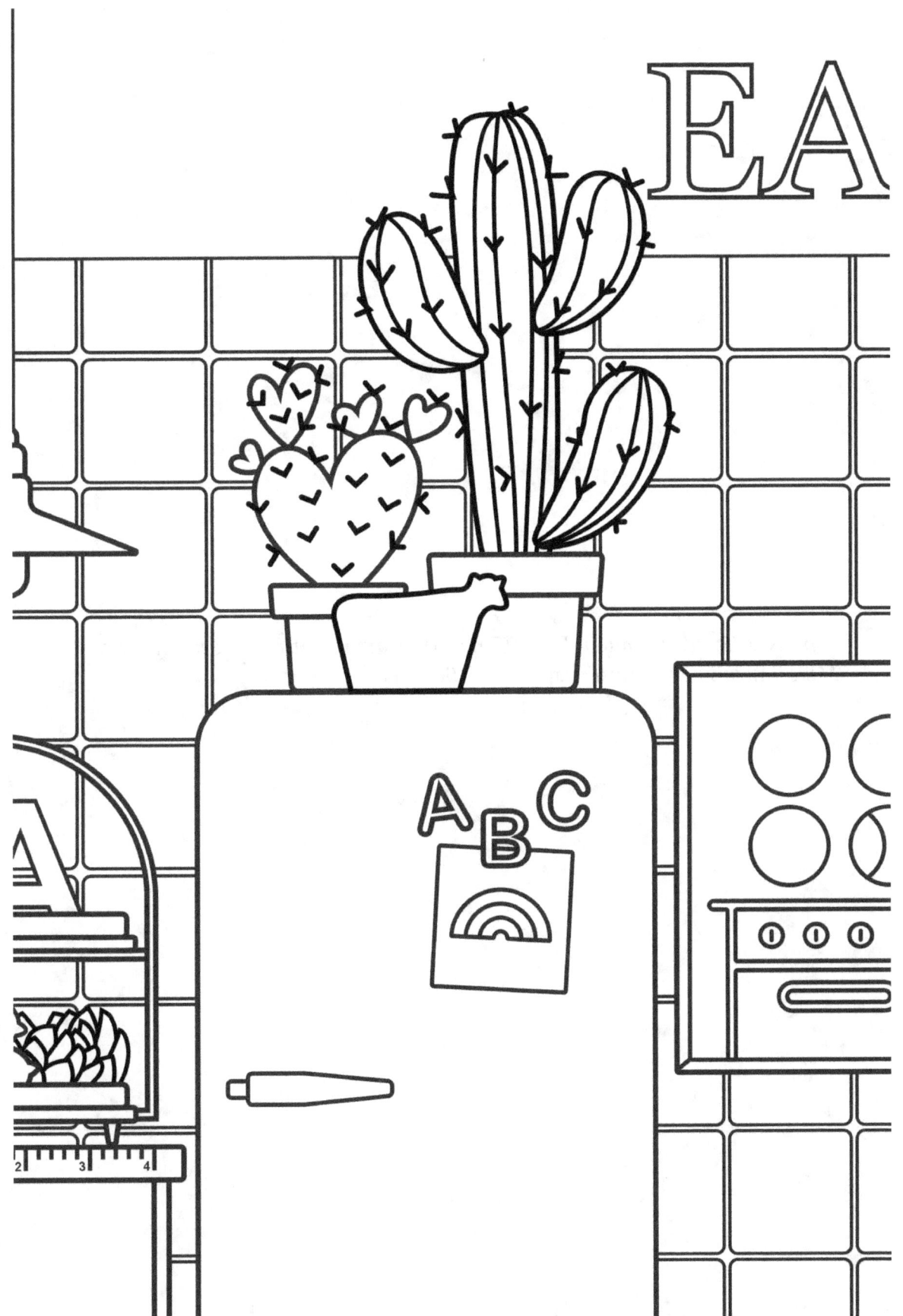

This is a Bleed Through Page. Find other great Titles by Searching for Mike Murphy on Your Favorite Book Retailer.

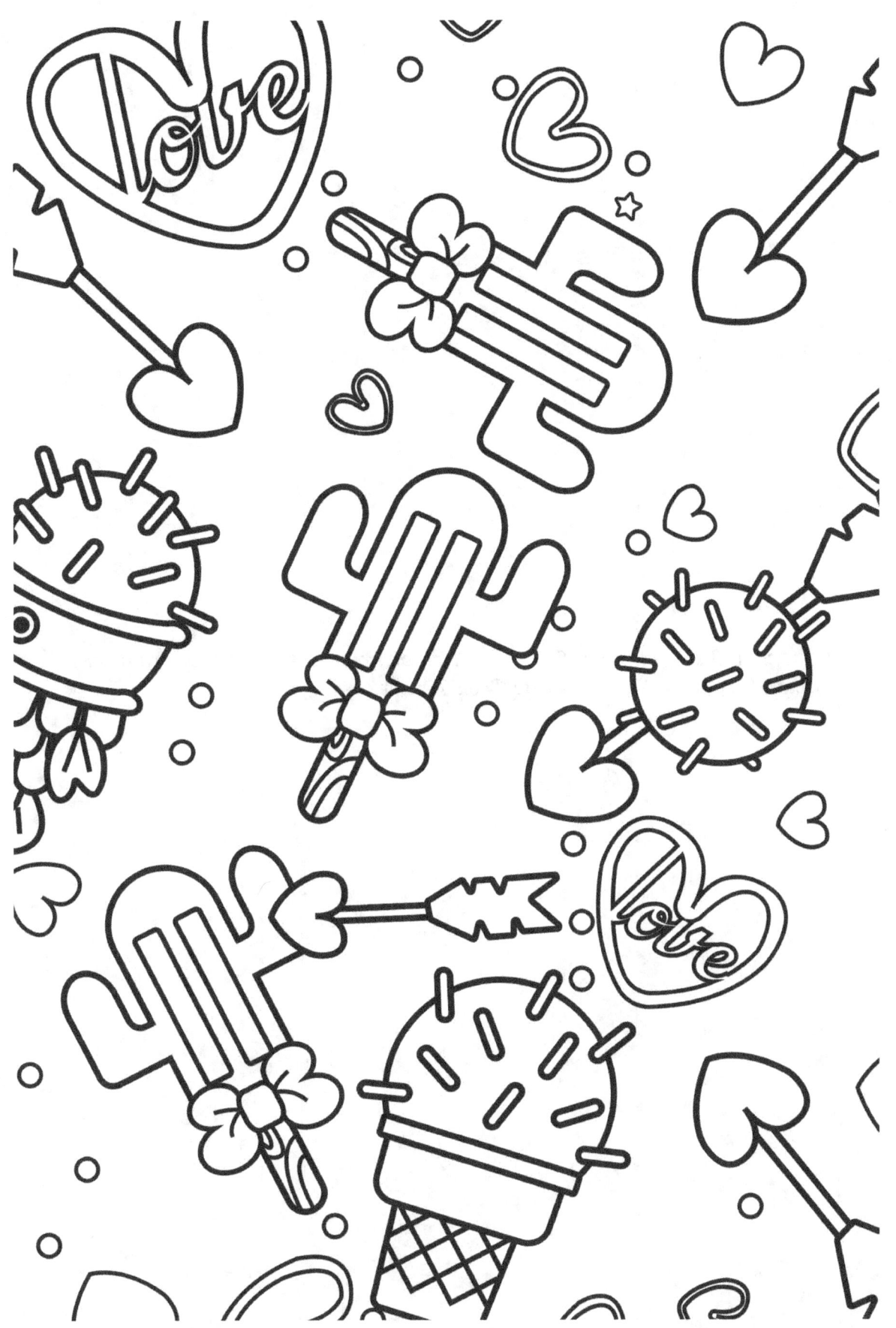

This is a Bleed Through Page. Find other great Titles by Searching for Mike Murphy on Your Favorite Book Retailer.

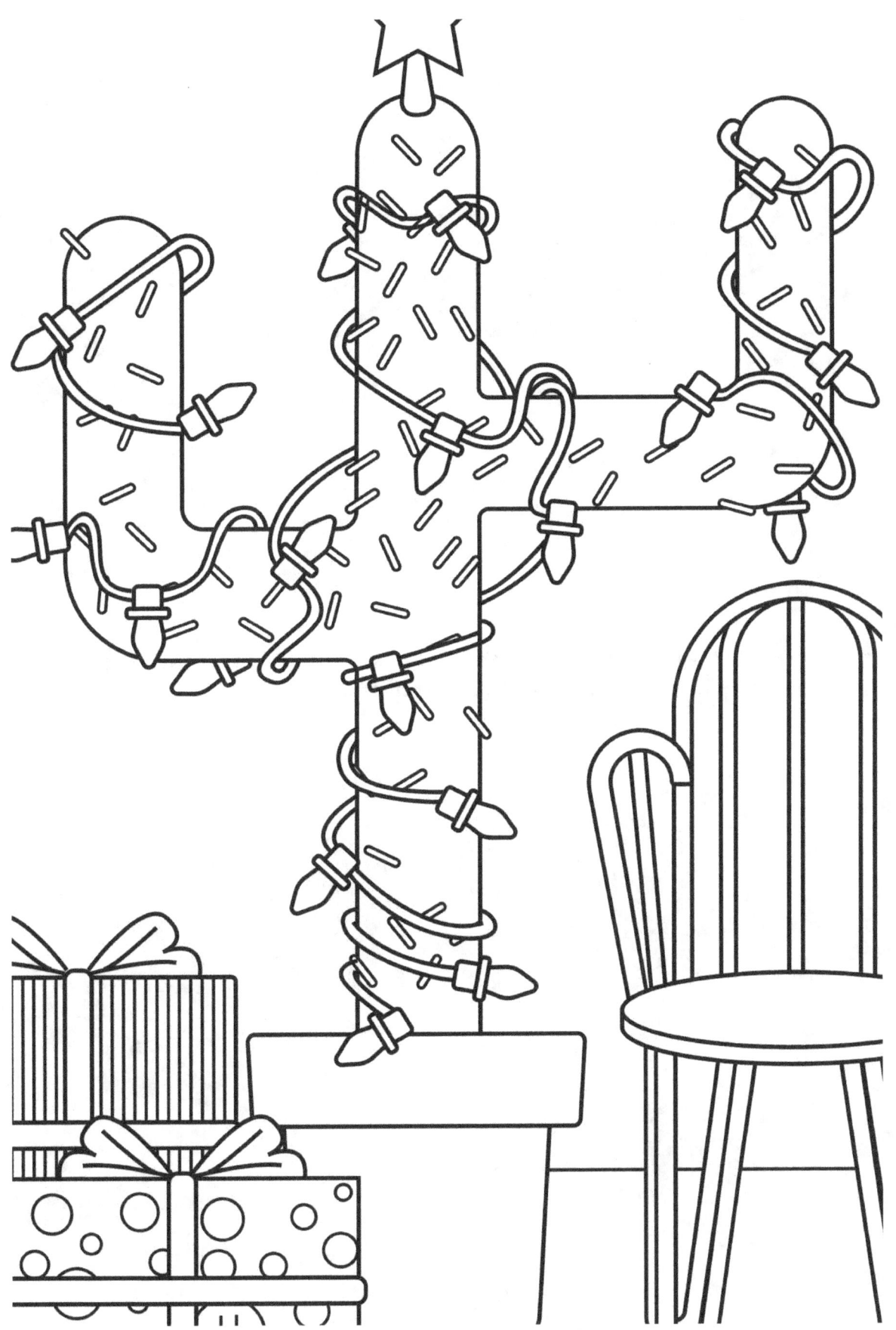

This is a Bleed Through Page. Find other great Titles by Searching for Mike Murphy on Your Favorite Book Retailer.

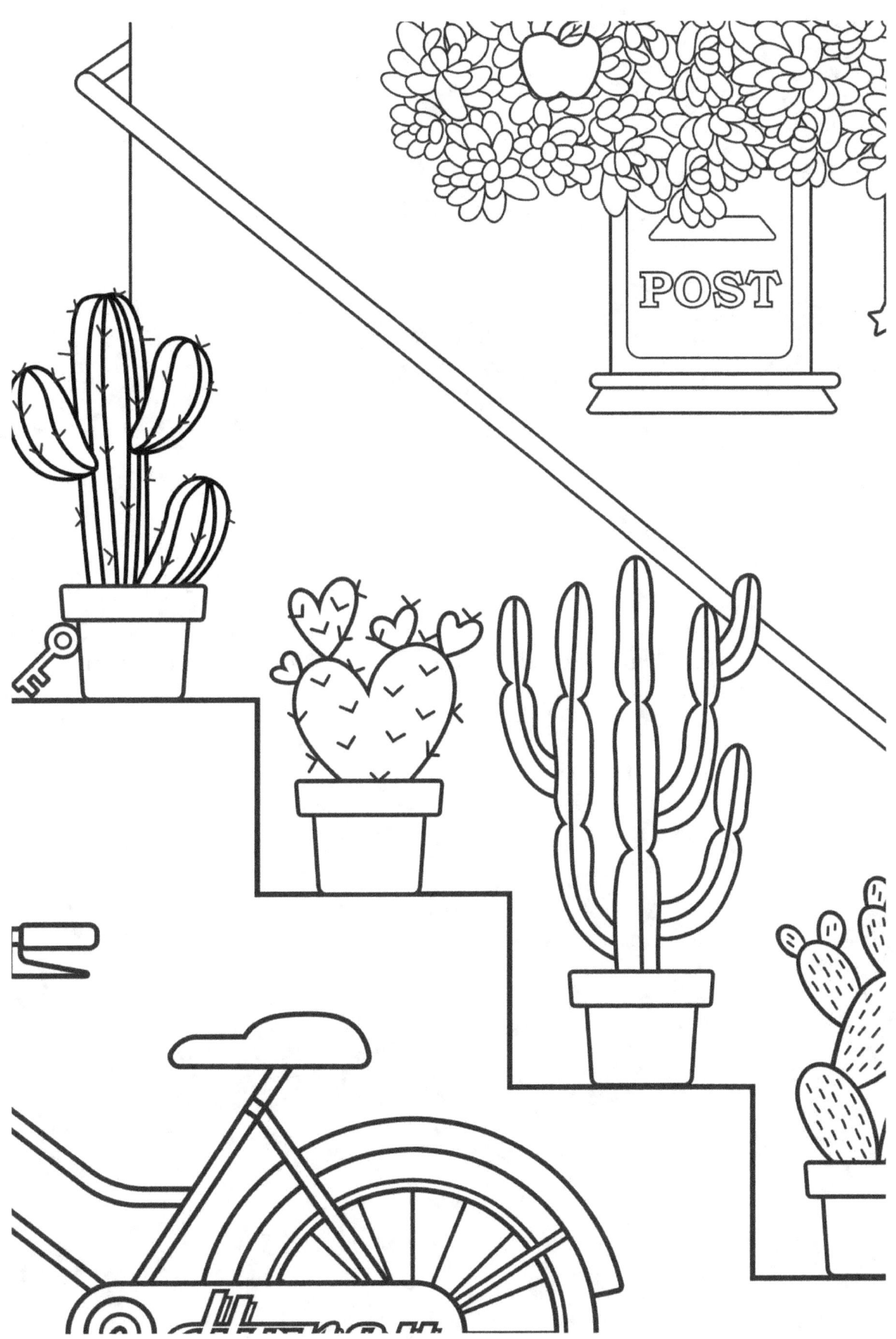

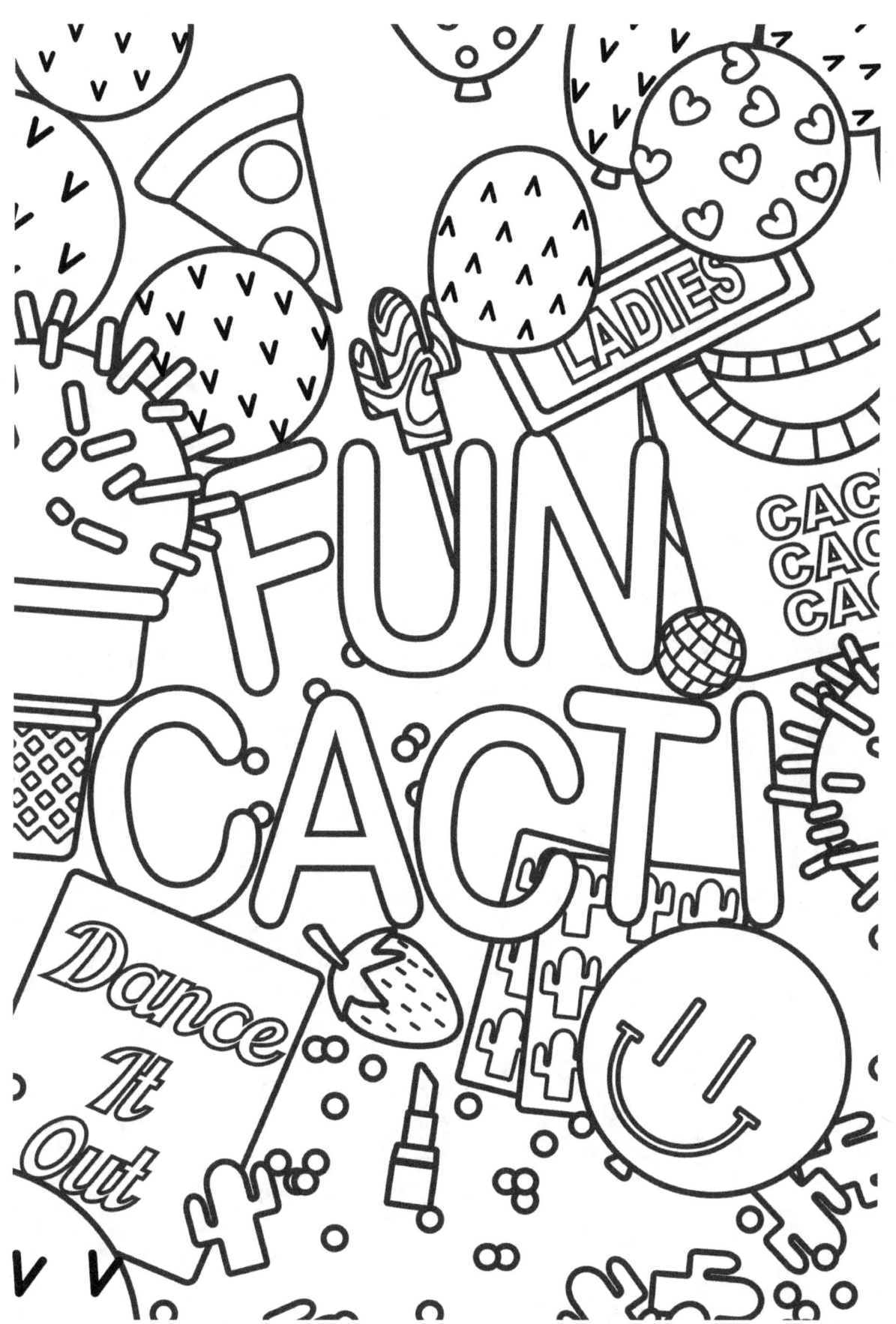

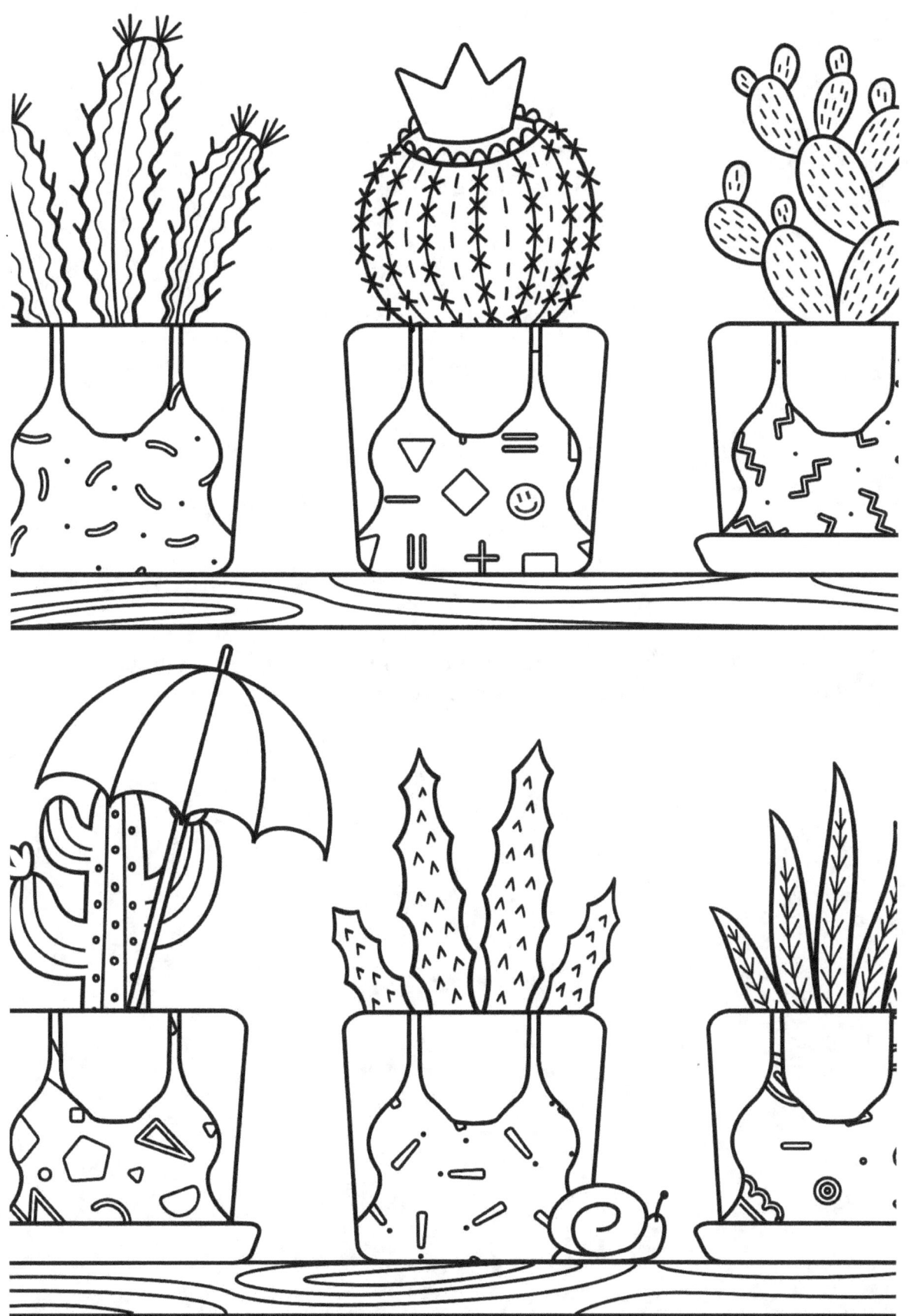

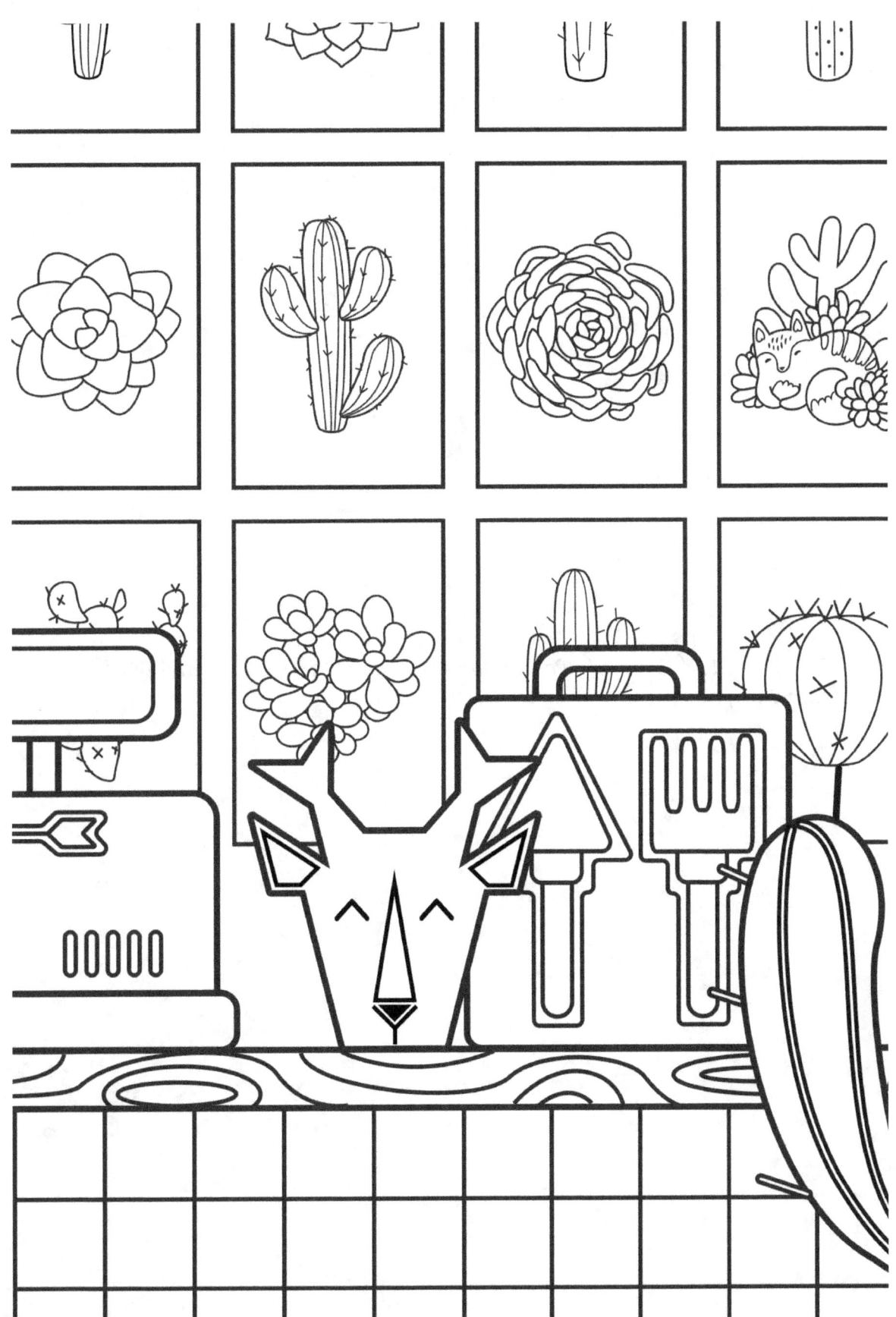

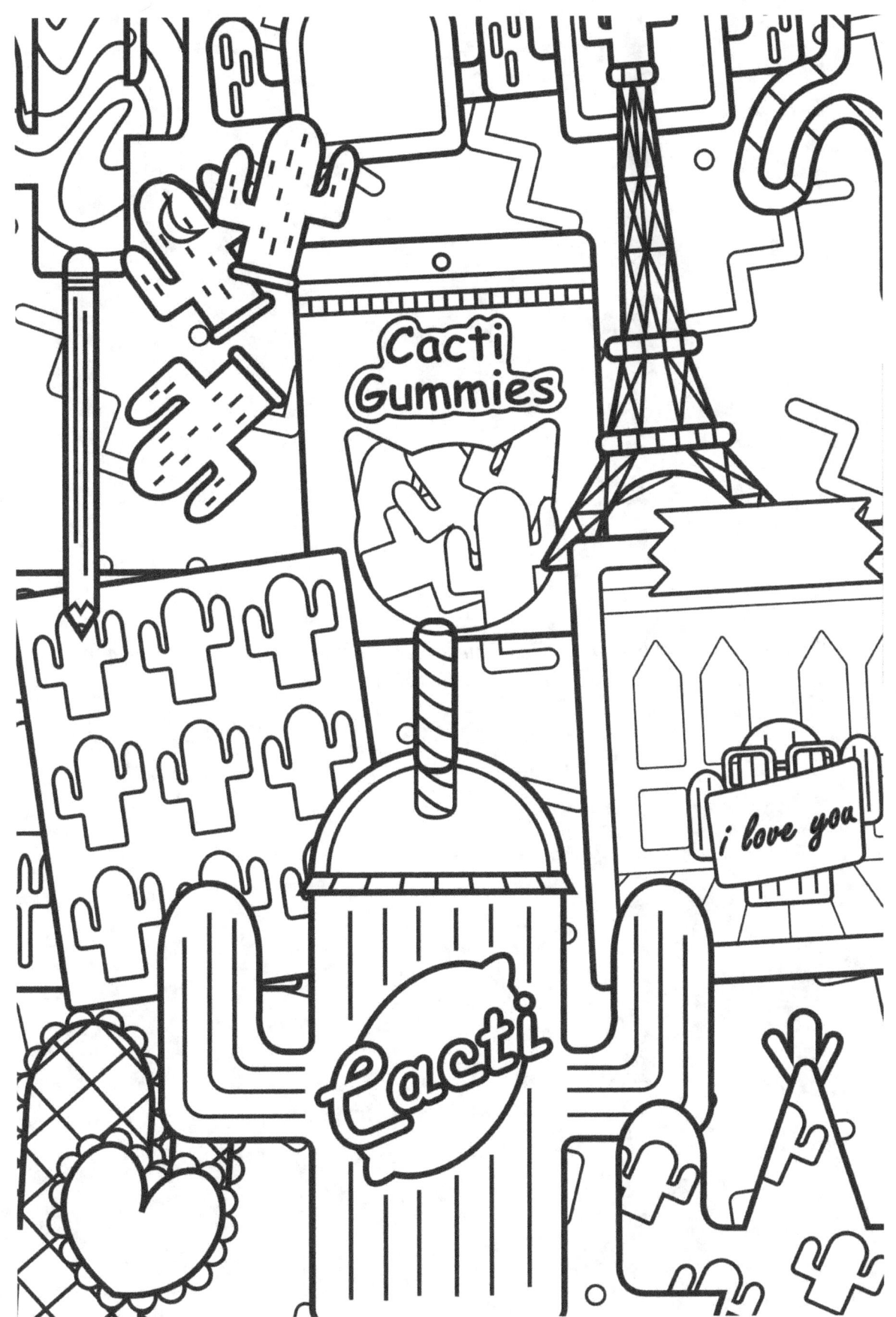

This is a Bleed Through Page. Find other great Titles by Searching for Mike Murphy on Your Favorite Book Retailer.

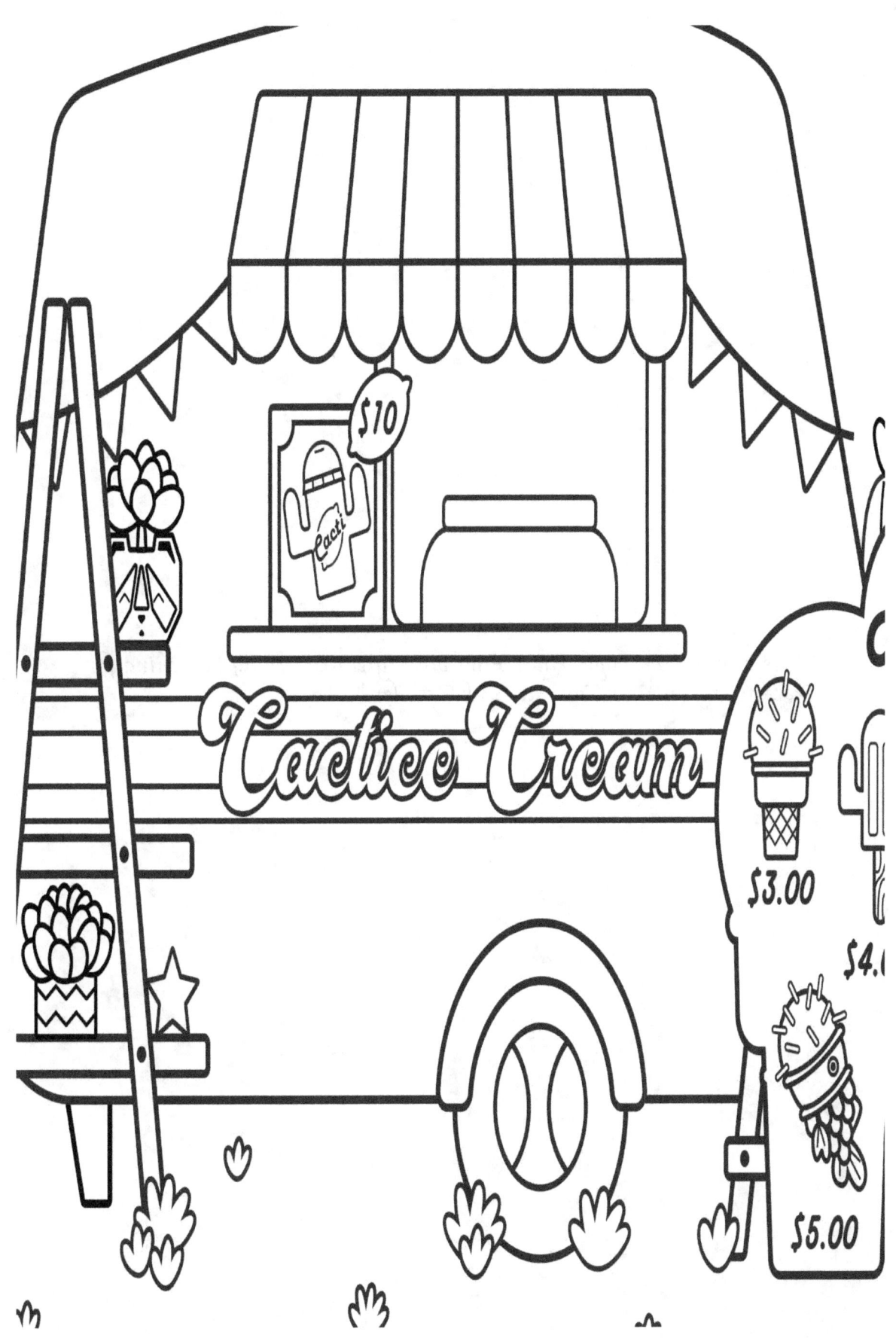

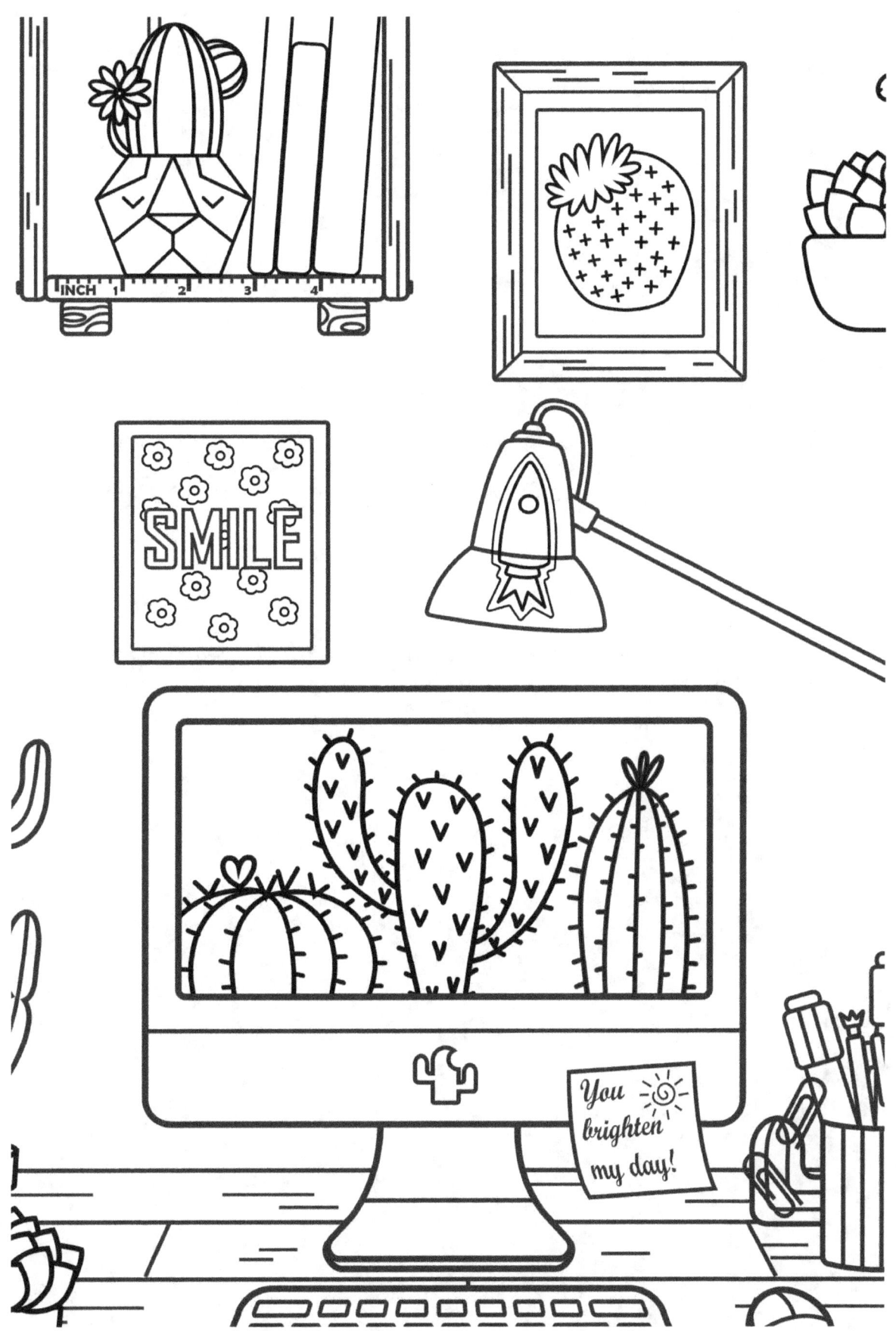

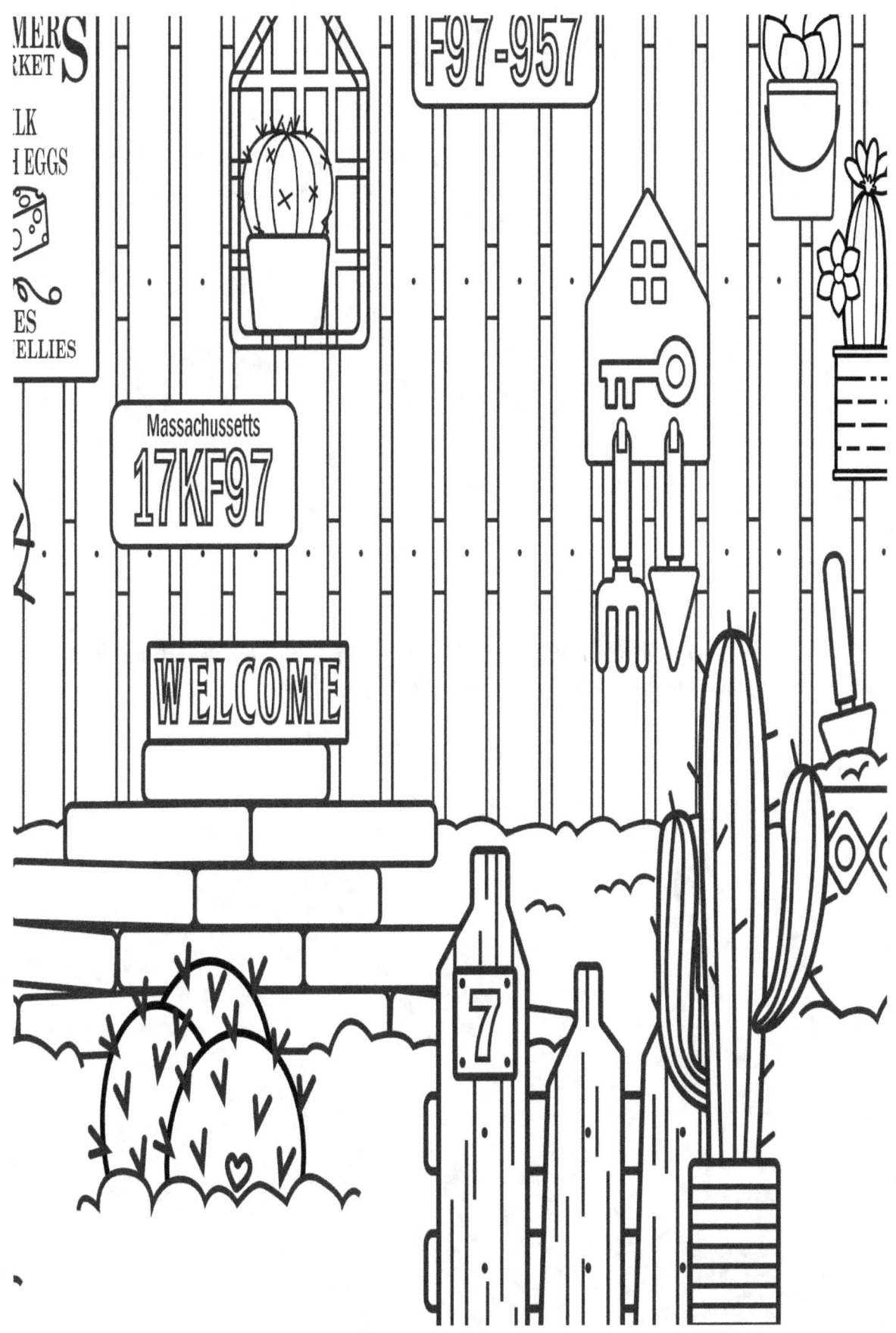

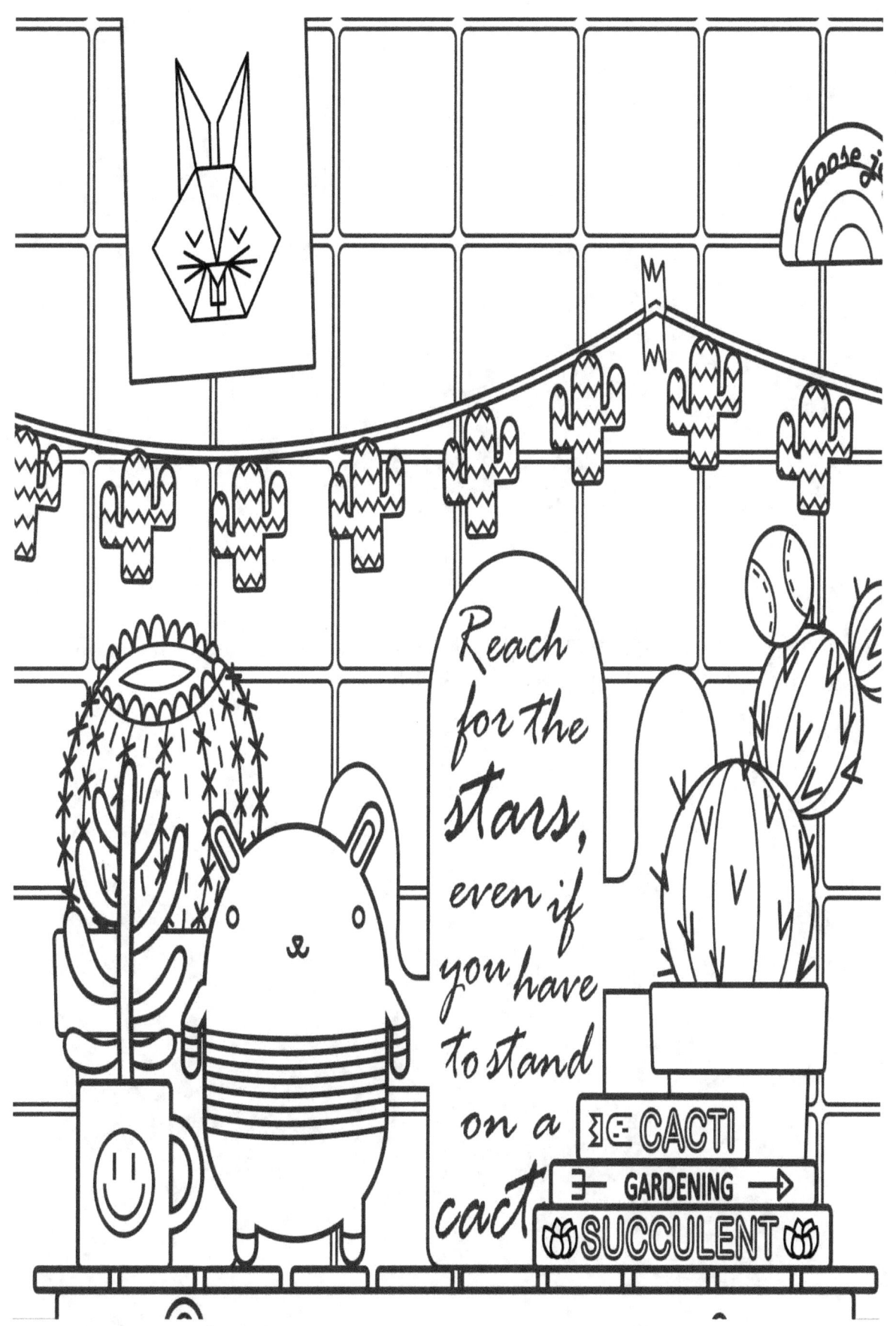

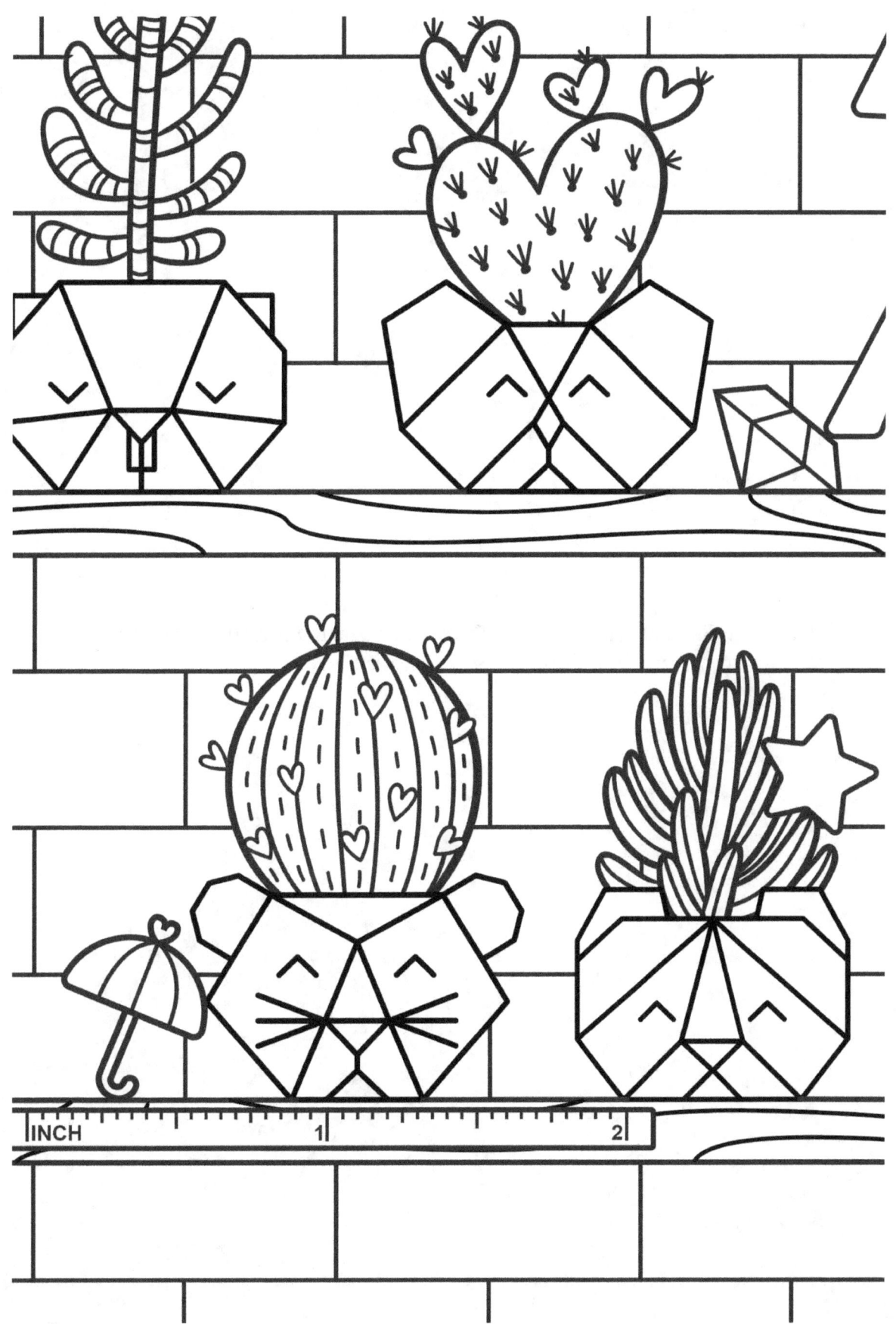

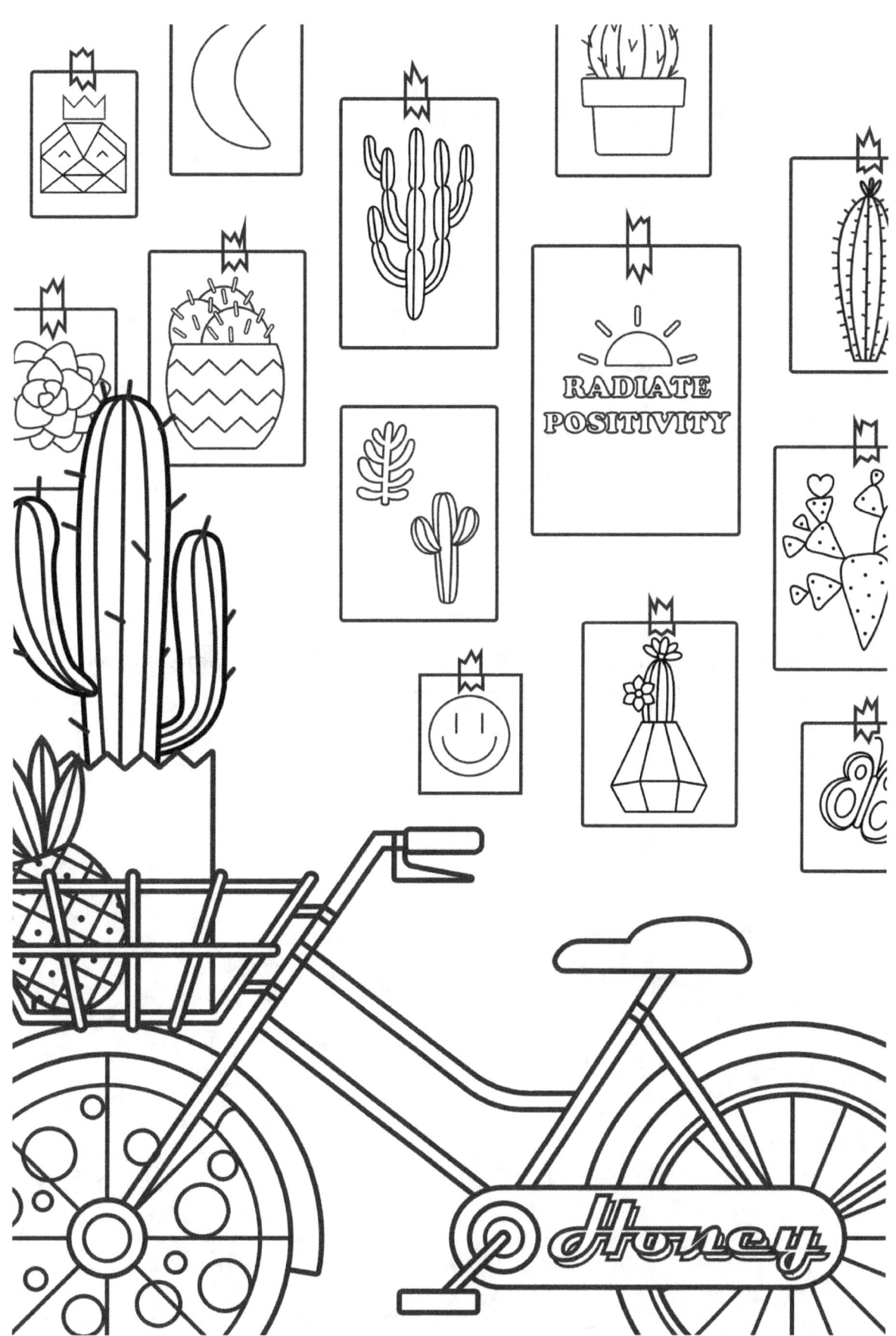

This is a Bleed Through Page. Find other great Titles by Searching for Mike Murphy on Your Favorite Book Retailer.

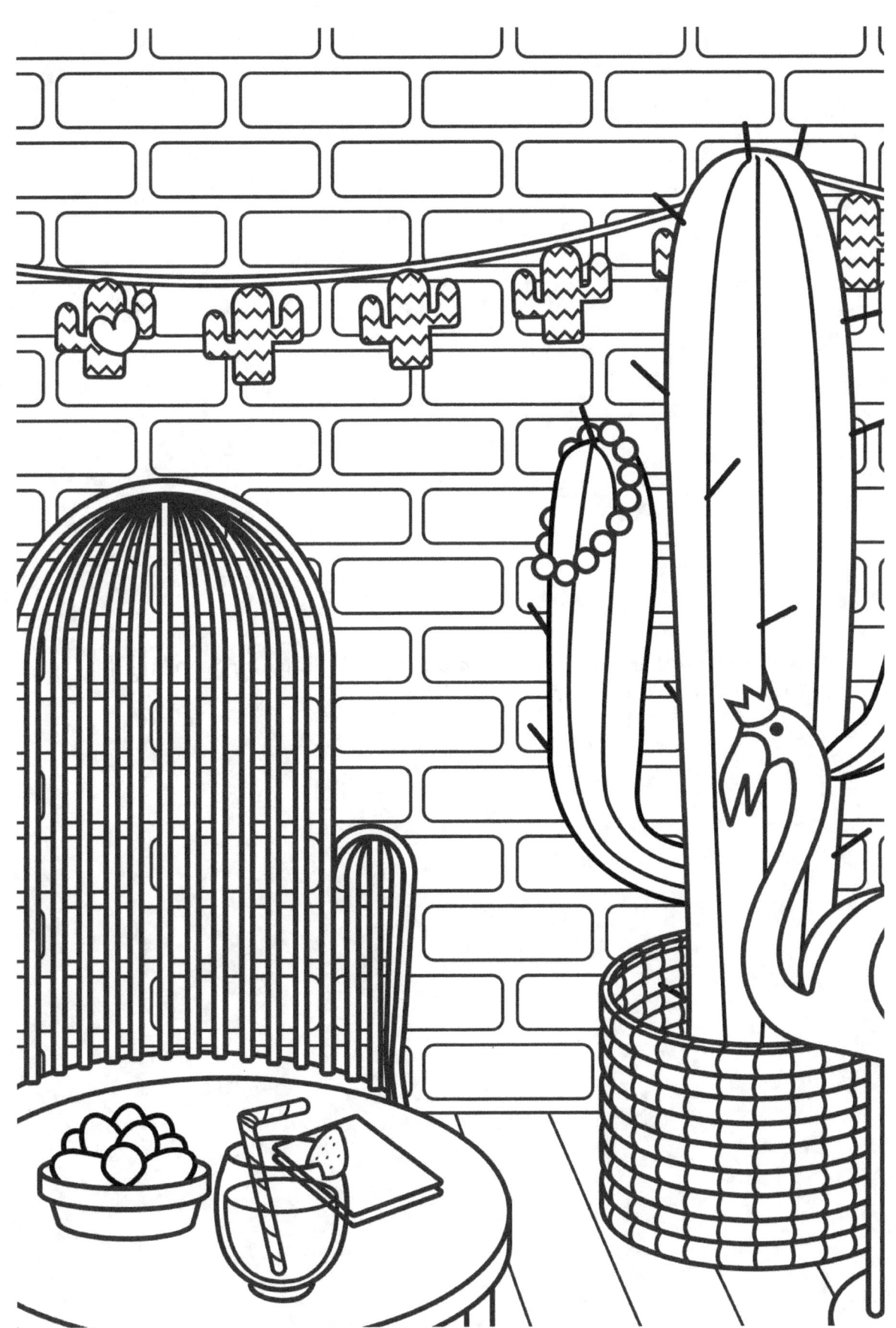

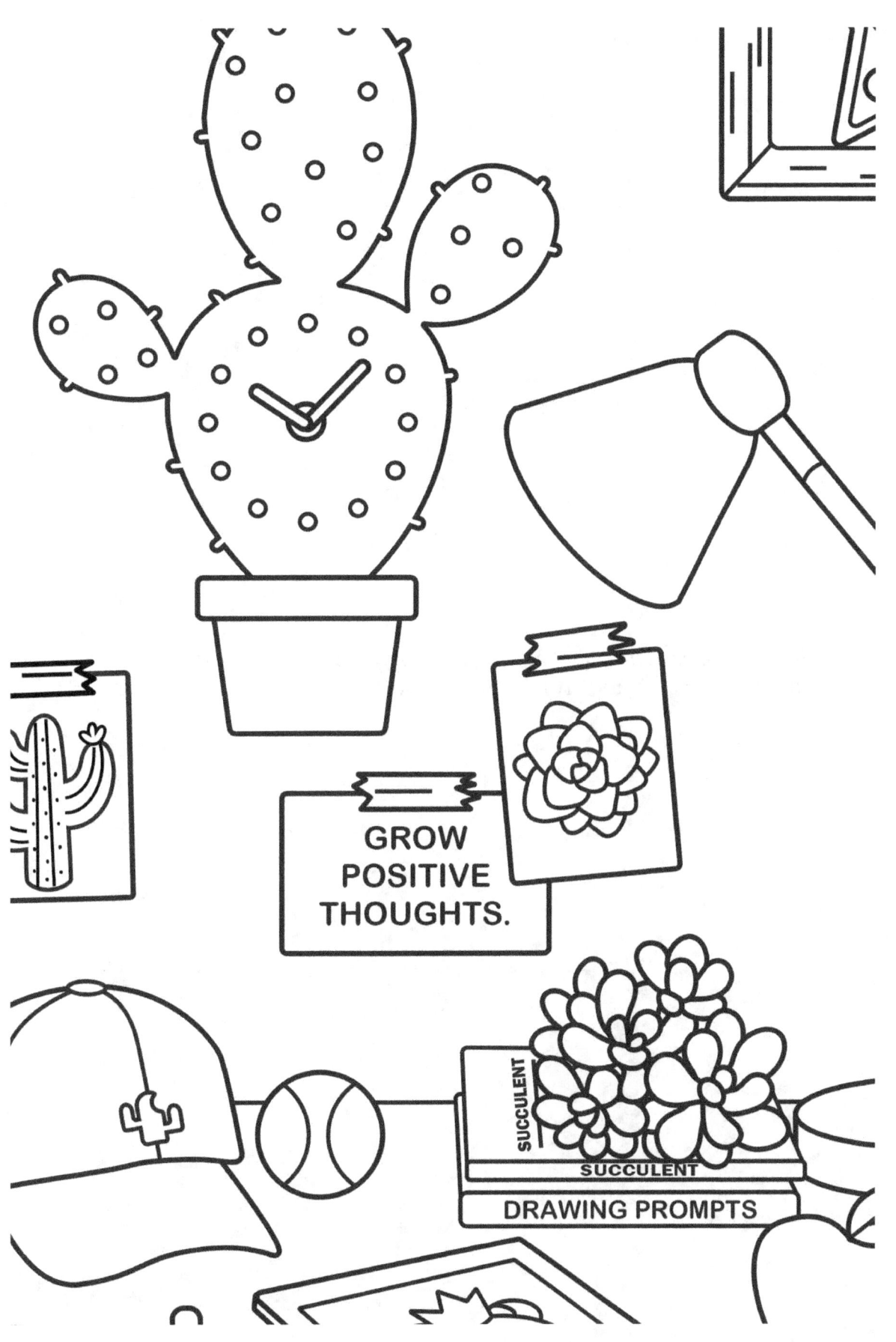

GROW
POSITIVE
THOUGHTS.

SUCCULENT

SUCCULENT

DRAWING PROMPTS

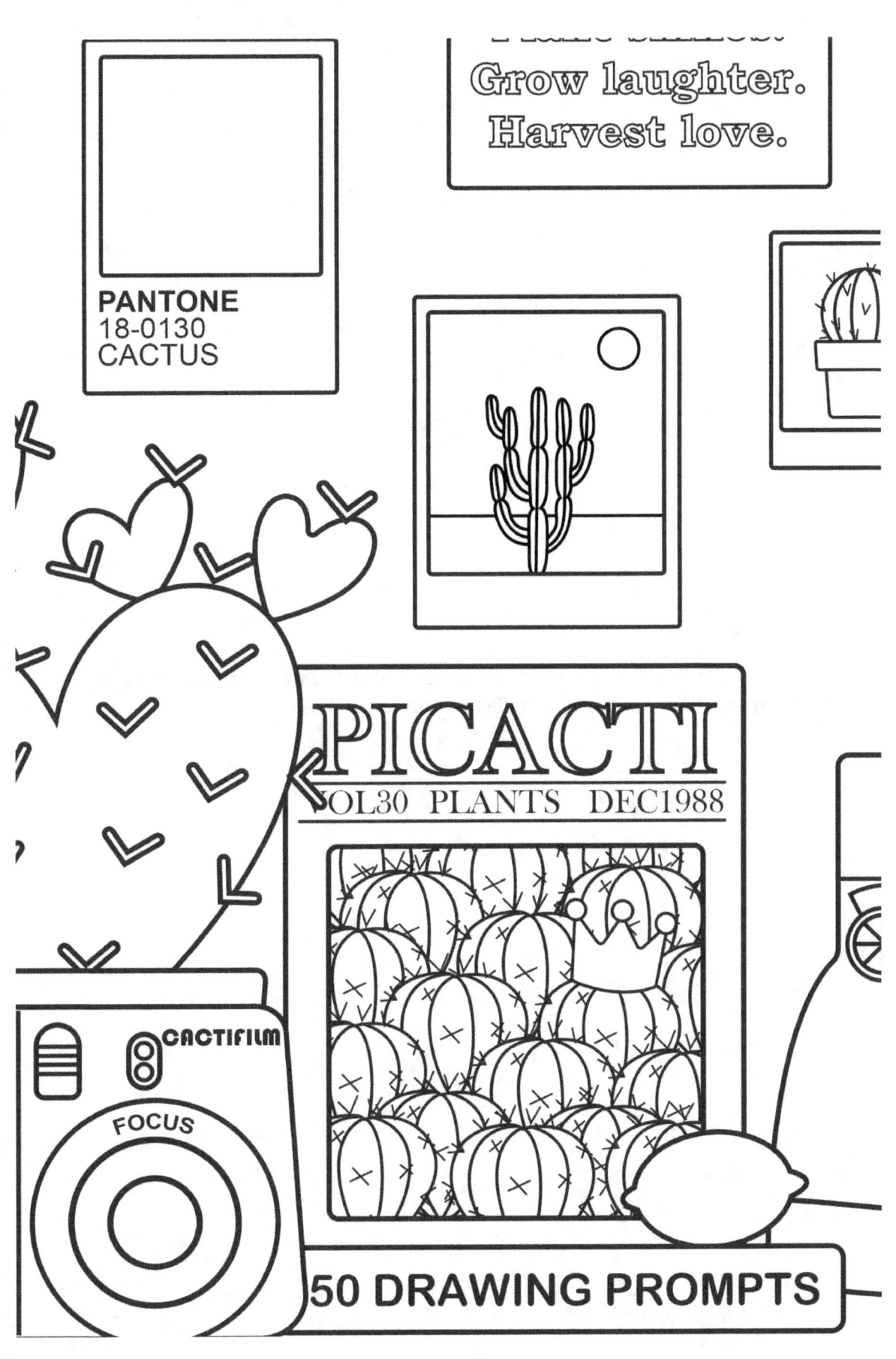

PANTONE
18-0130
CACTUS

Grow laughter.
Harvest love.

PICACTI
OL30 PLANTS DEC1988

CACTIFILM

FOCUS

50 DRAWING PROMPTS

This is a Bleed Through Page. Find other great Titles by Searching for Mike Murphy on Your Favorite Book Retailer.

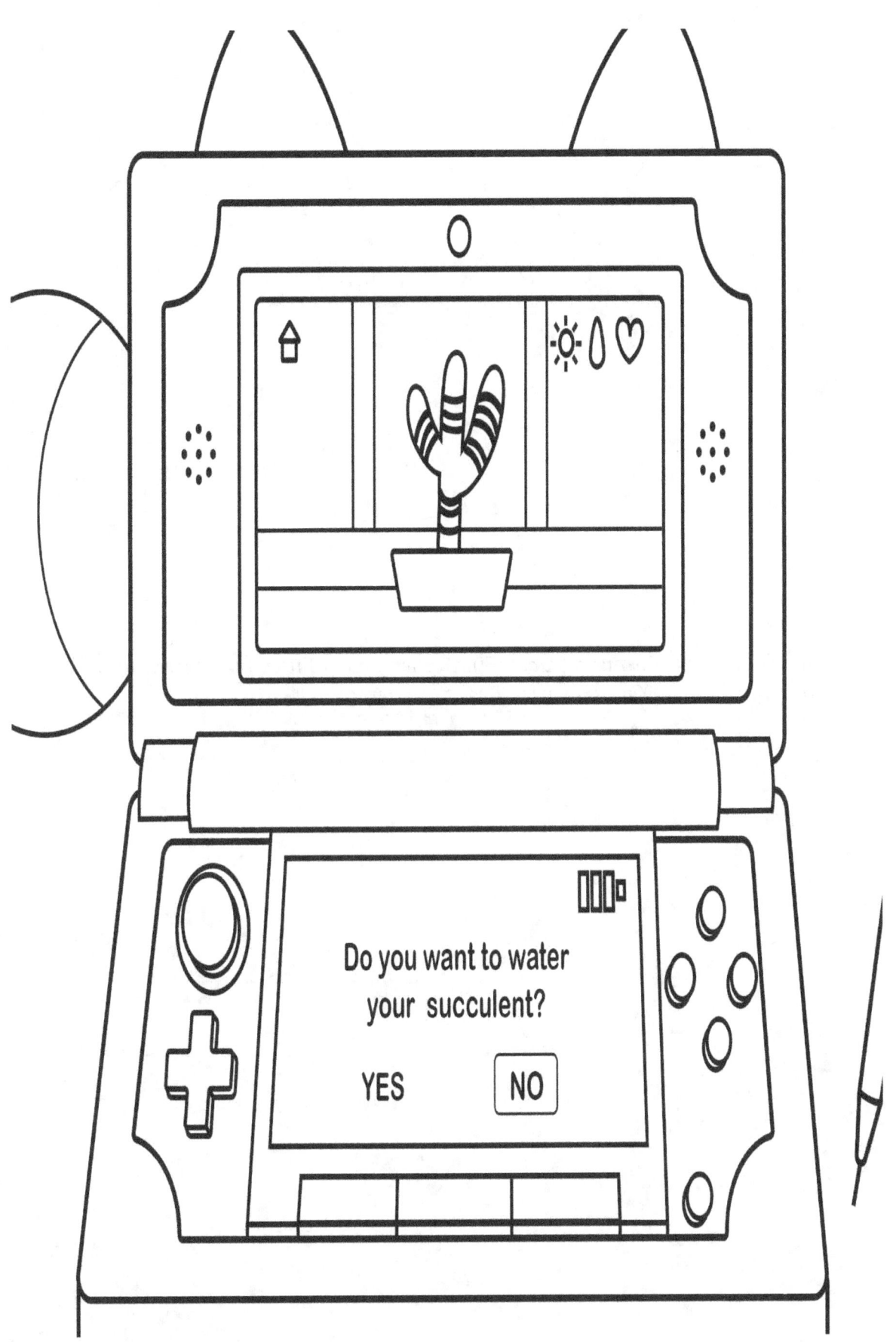

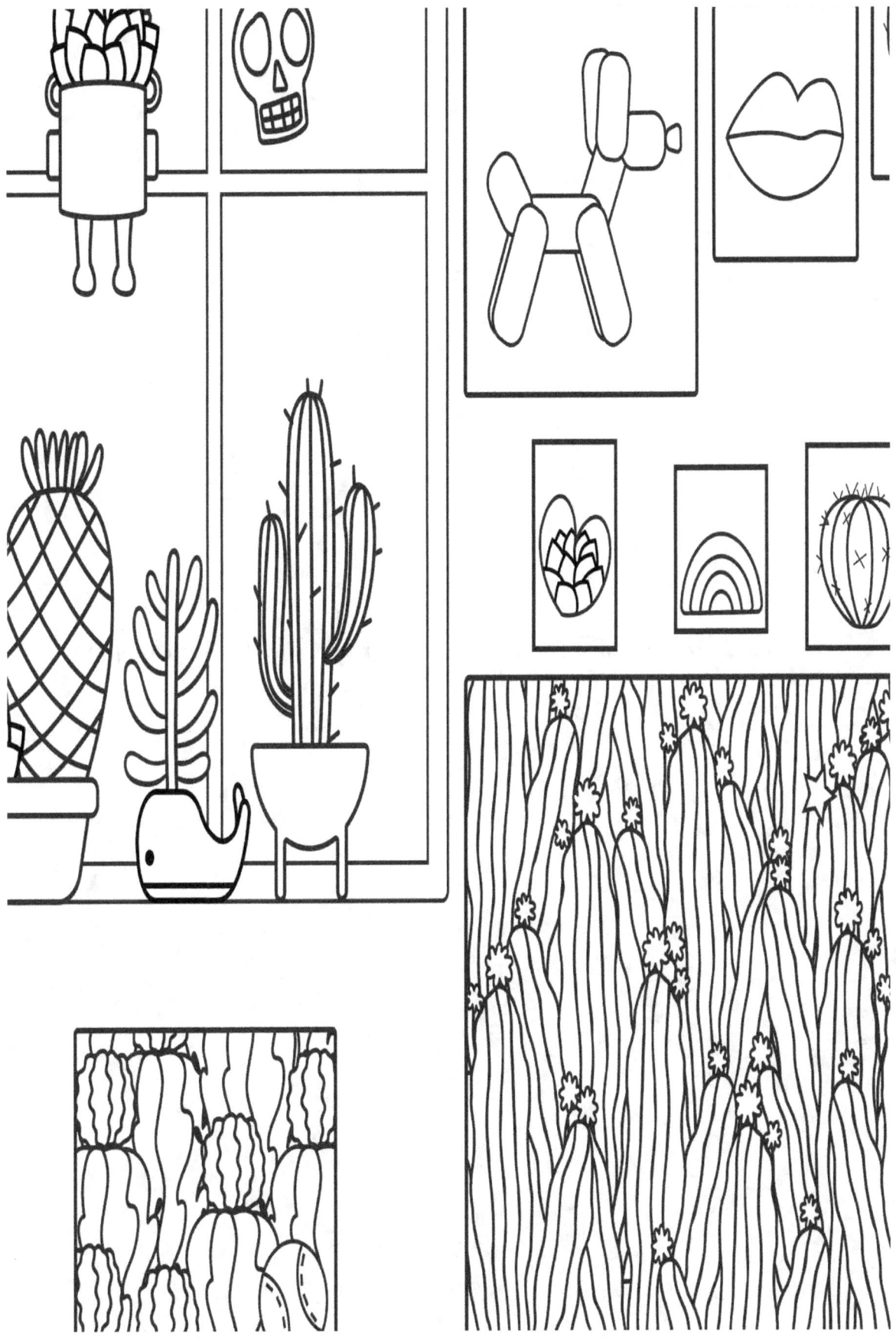

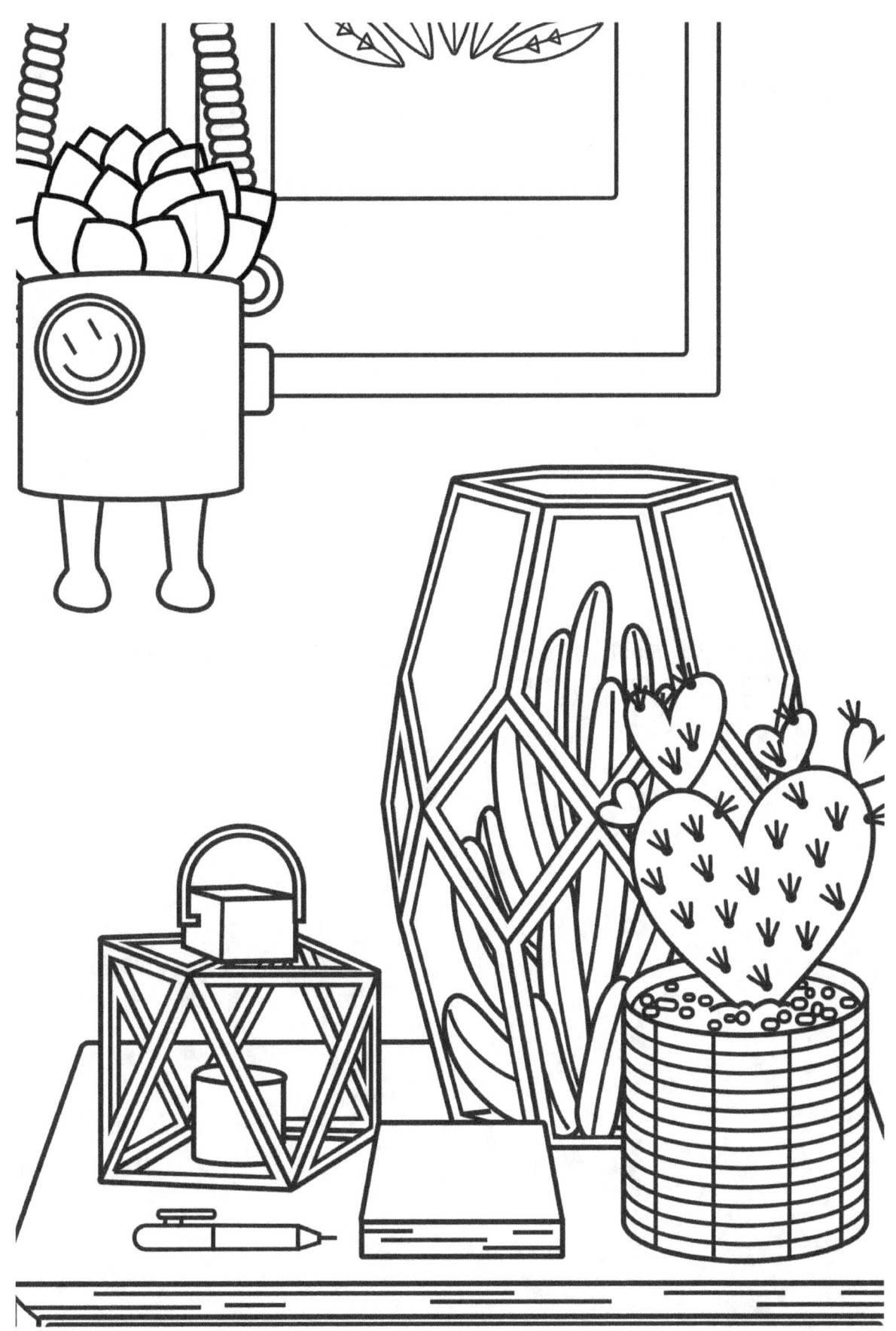

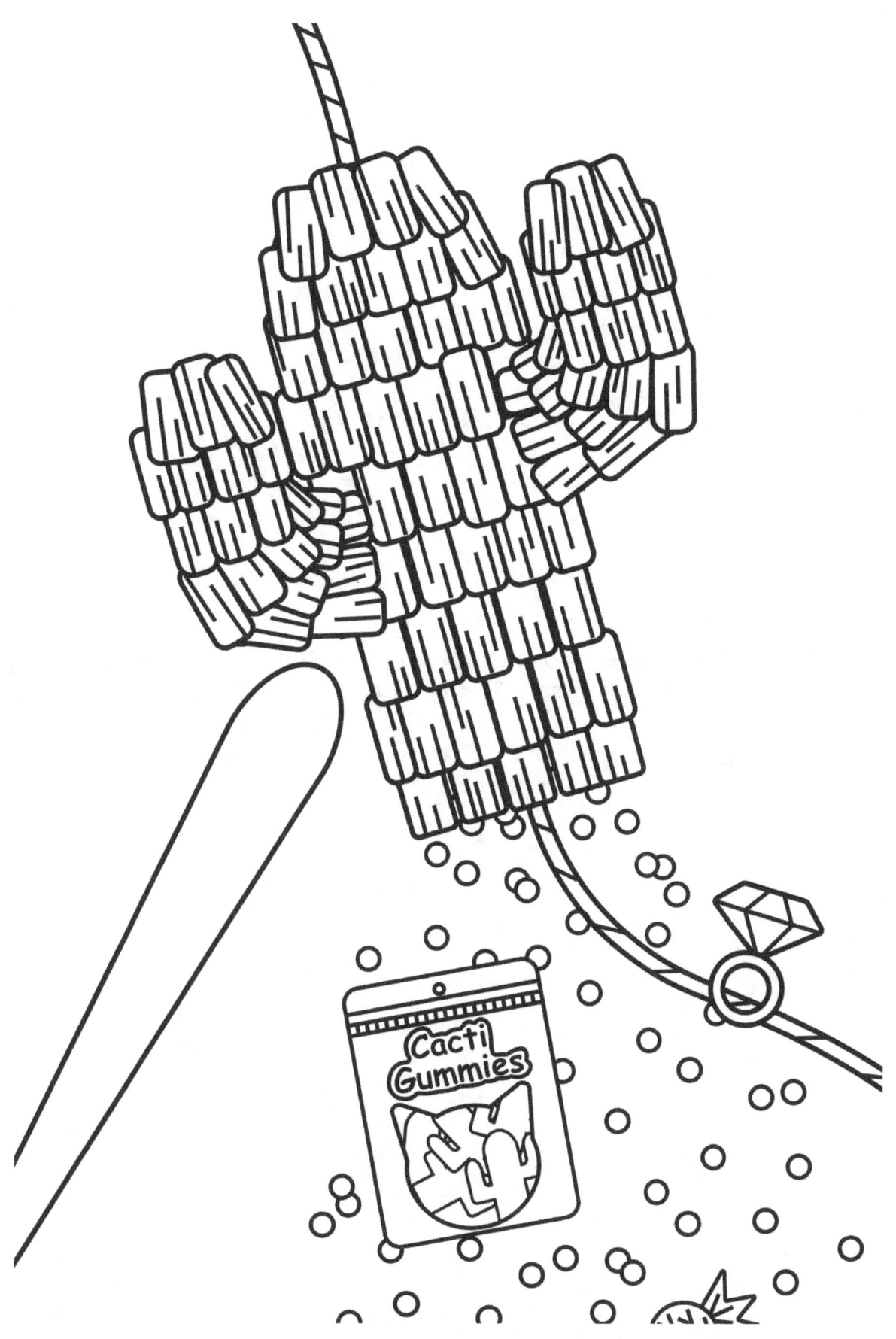

This is a Bleed Through Page. Find other great Titles by Searching for Mike Murphy on Your Favorite Book Retailer.

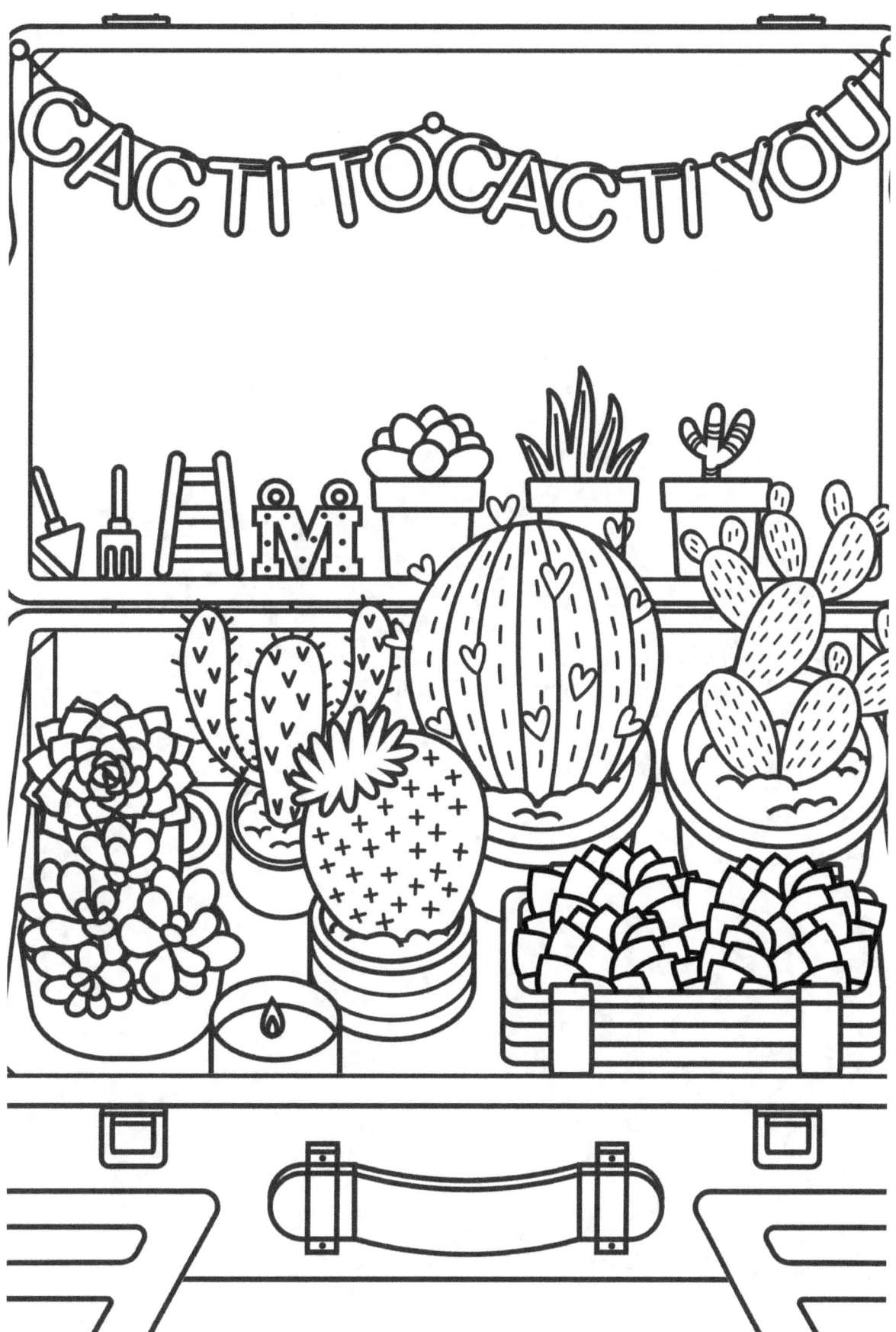

This is a Bleed Through Page. Find other great Titles by Searching for Mike Murphy on Your Favorite Book Retailer.

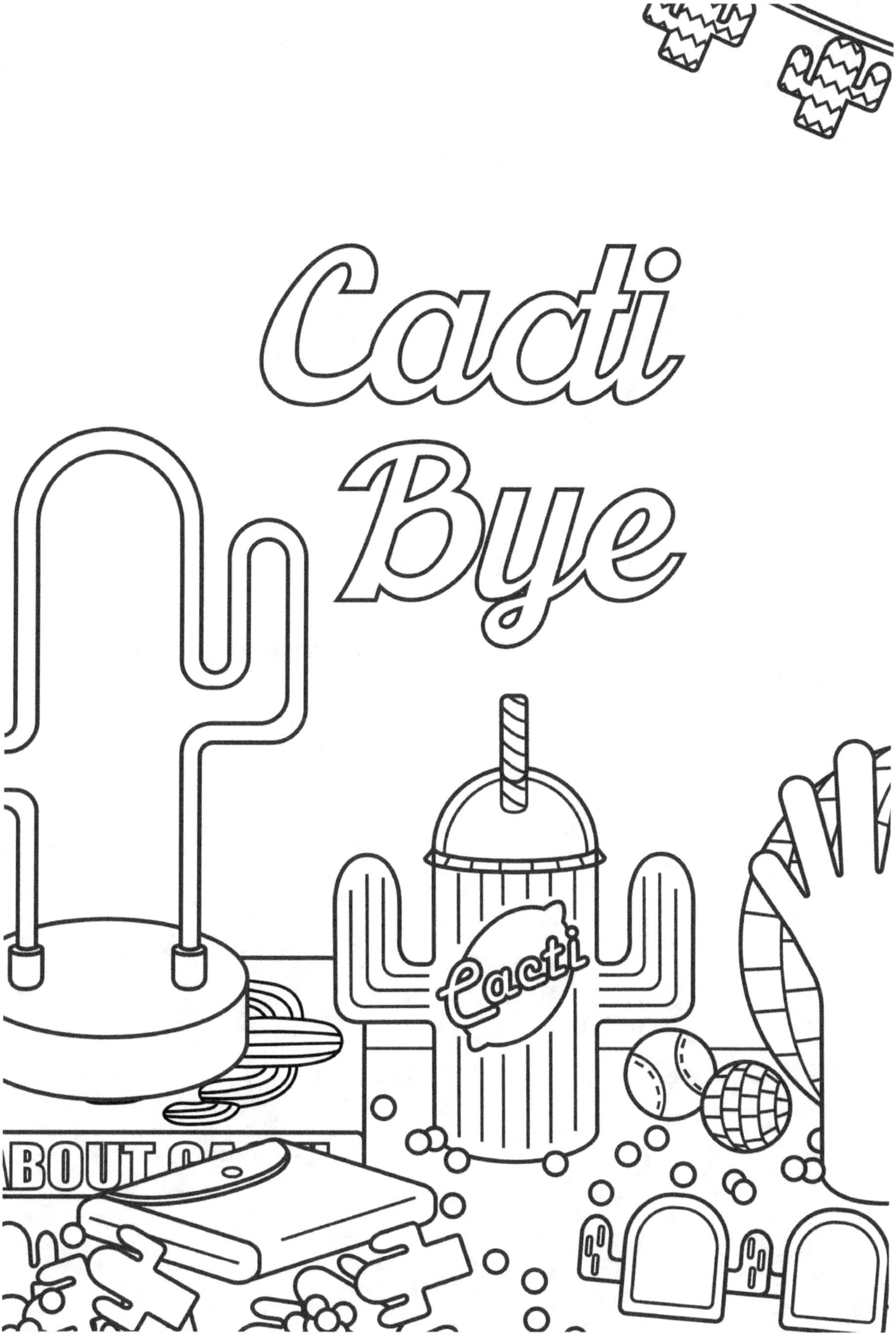

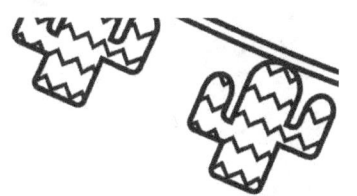

Cacti Bye

This is a Bleed Through Page. Find other great Titles by Searching for Mike Murphy on Your Favorite Book Retailer.

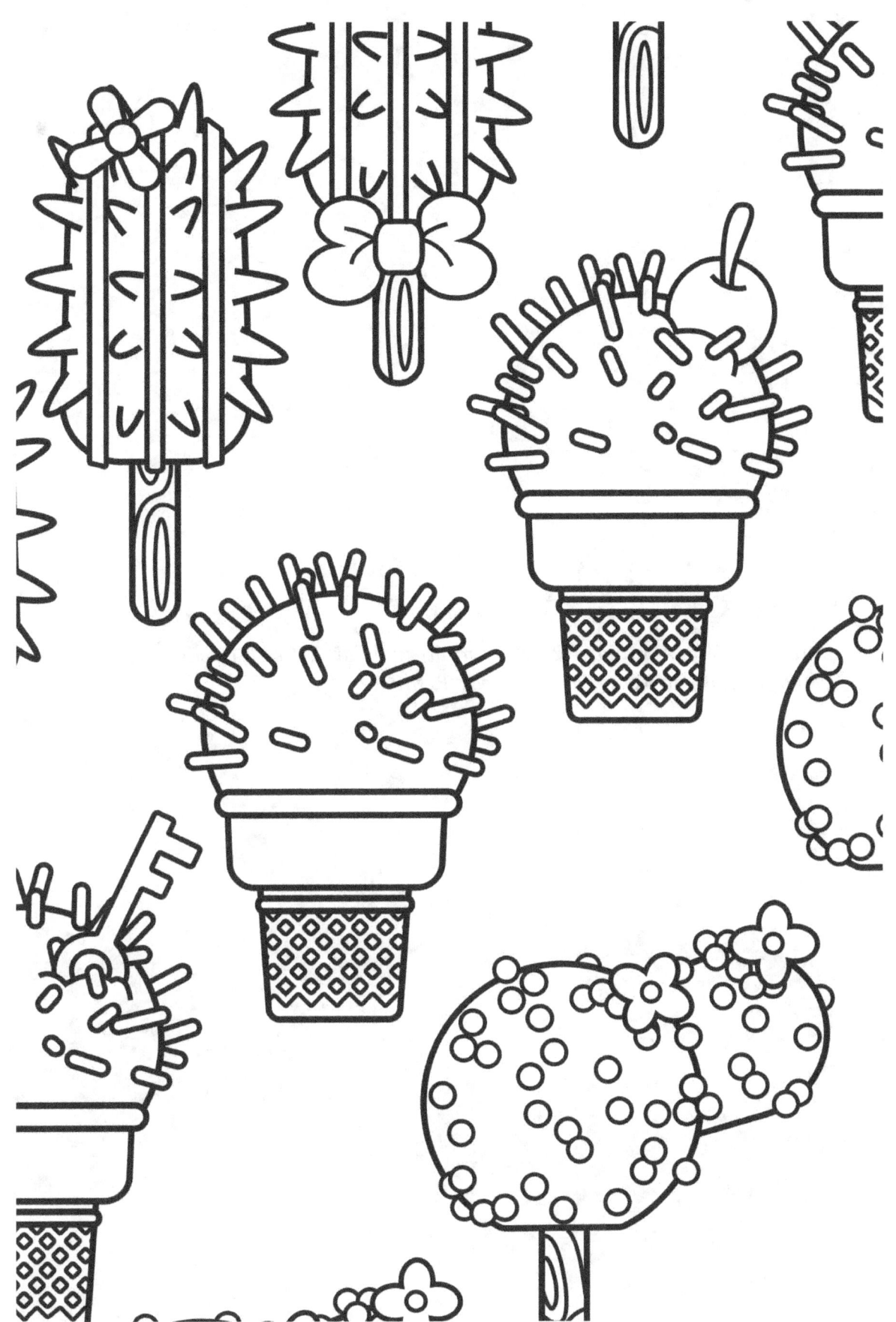

Succulent Treasures
Cacti Box
How to care for Cactus Garden

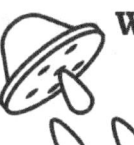

Water
Summer: Once a week
Winter: Once a month
Put the water in the soil,
not directly on the plant.

Soil
Use Good quality potting soil and
and change it every year. Also make
sure that has an appropriate drainage.

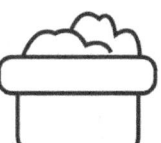

Sun
4 to 5 hours of direct
sunlight a day.

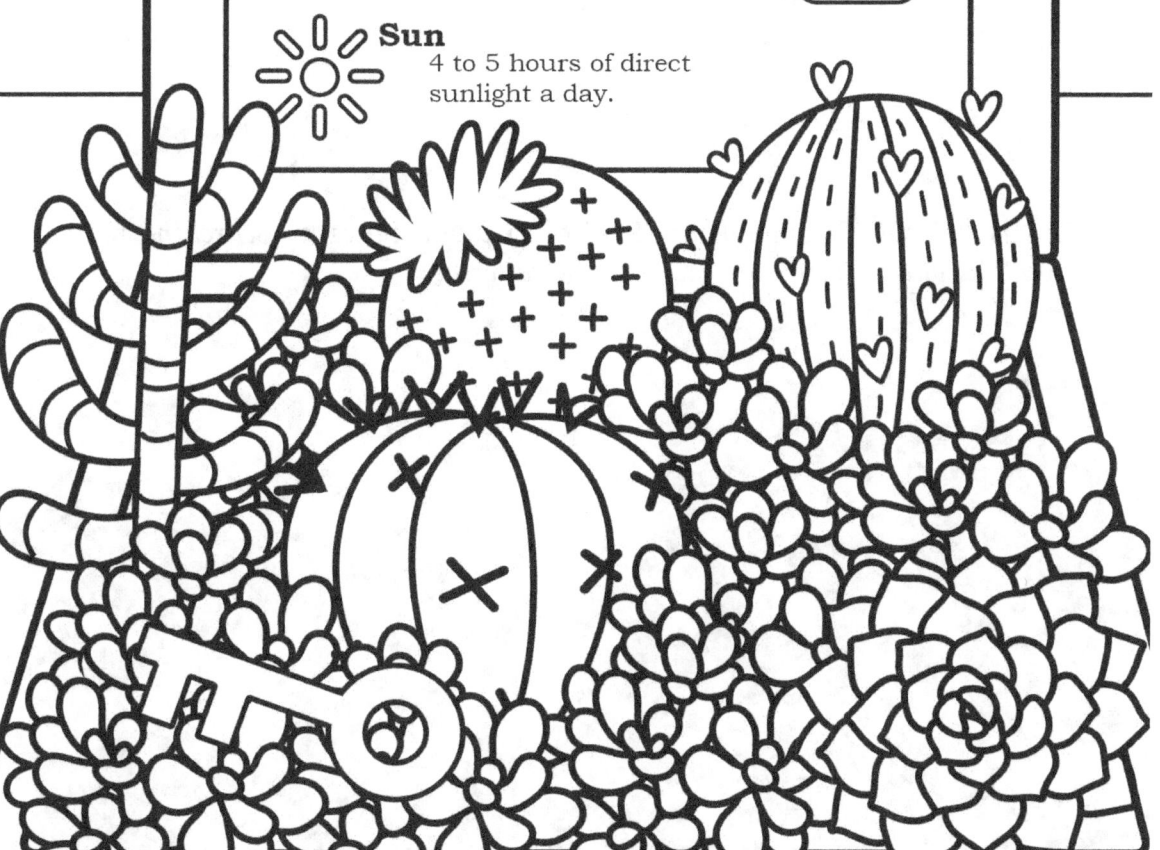

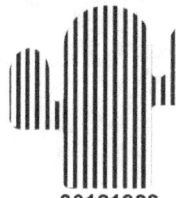

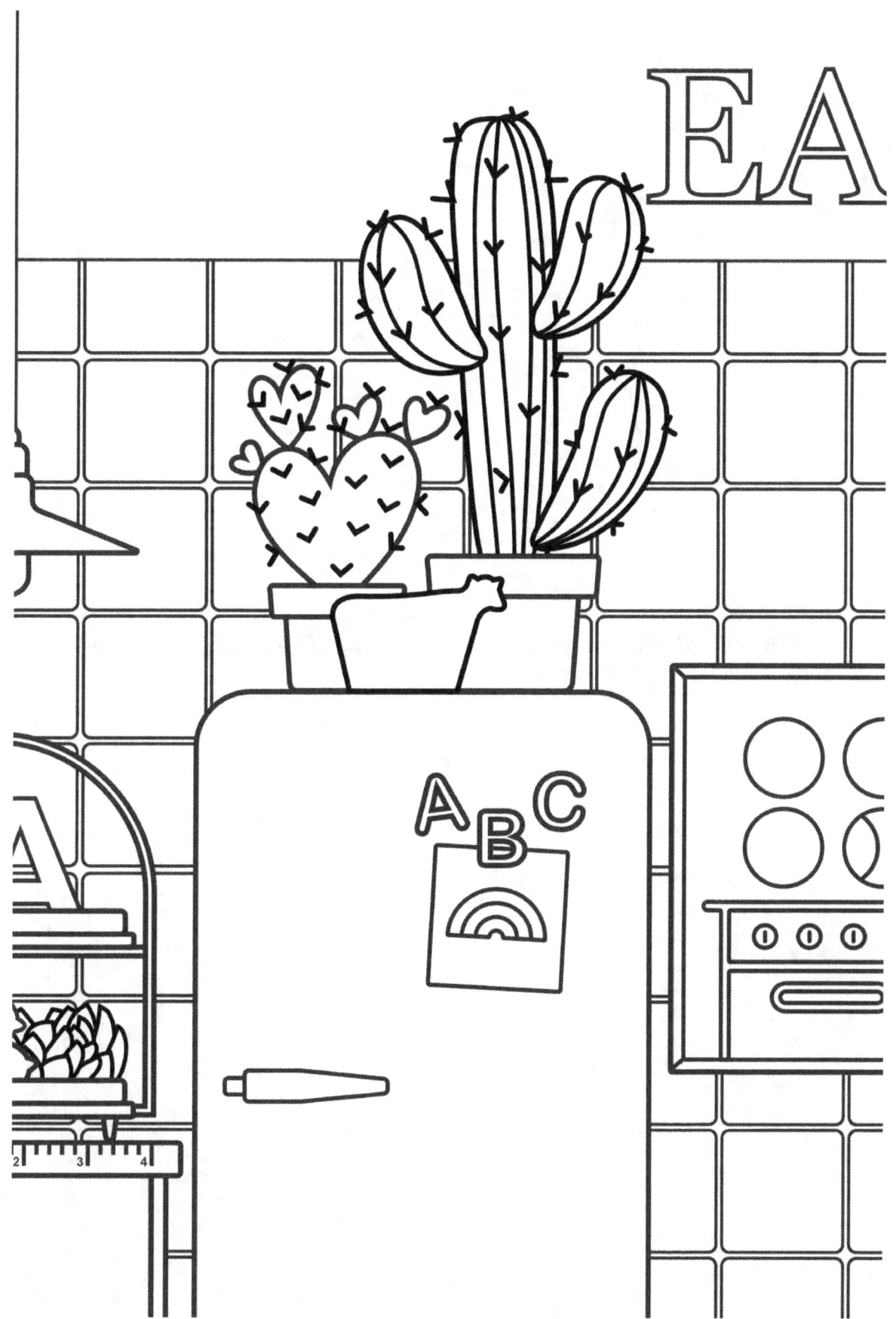

This is a Bleed Through Page. Find other great Titles by Searching for Mike Murphy on Your Favorite Book Retailer.

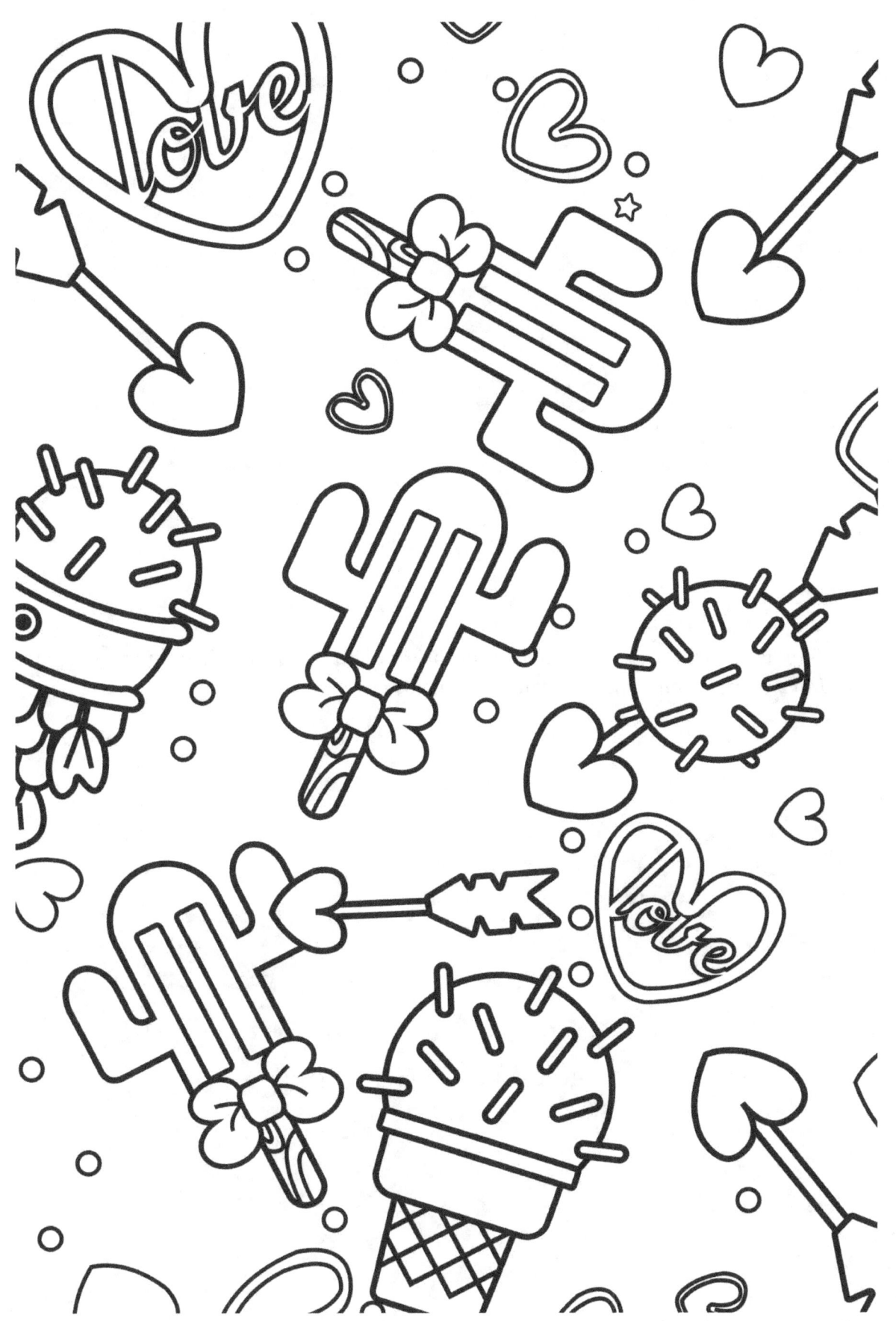

This is a Bleed Through Page. Find other great Titles by Searching for Mike Murphy on Your Favorite Book Retailer.

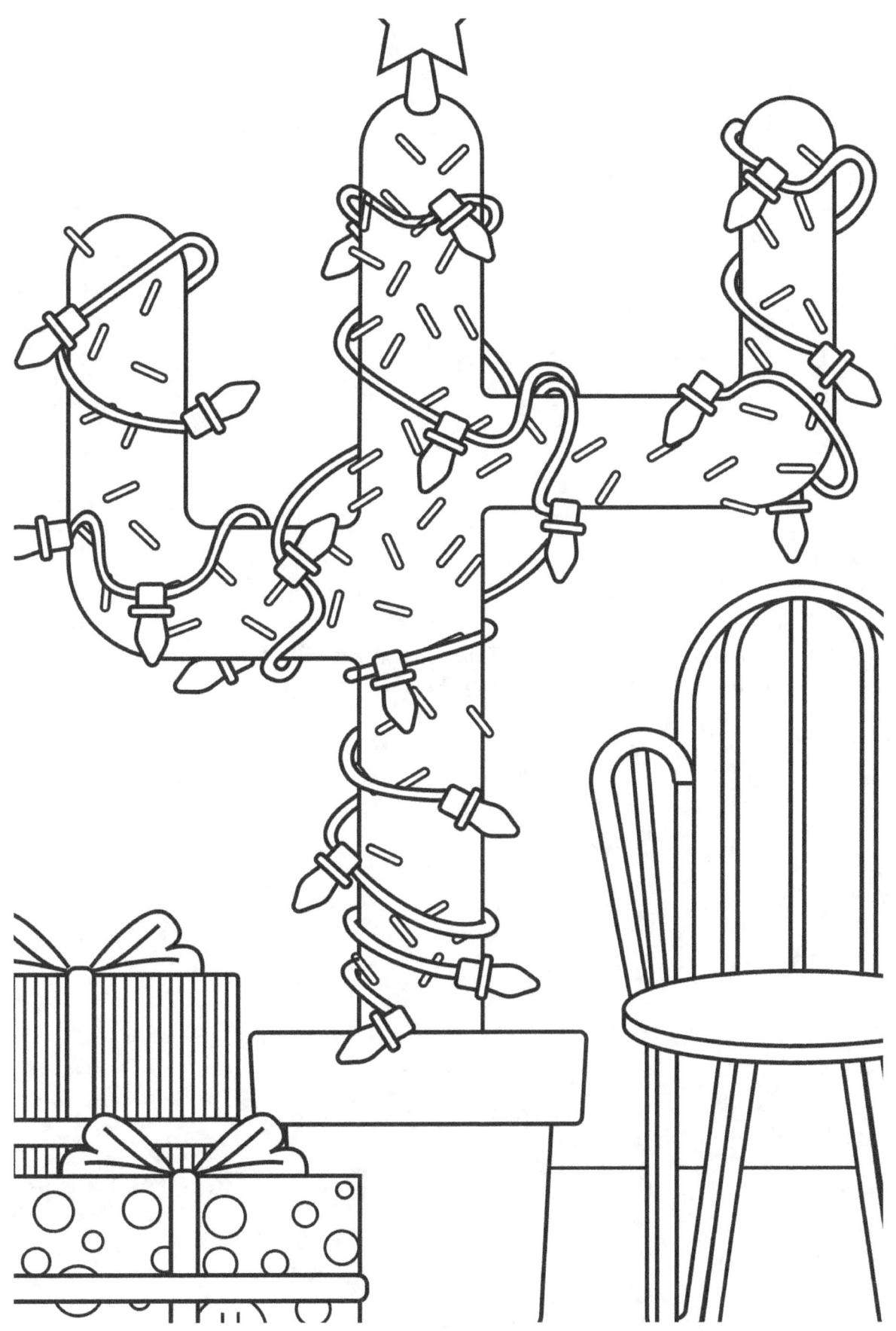

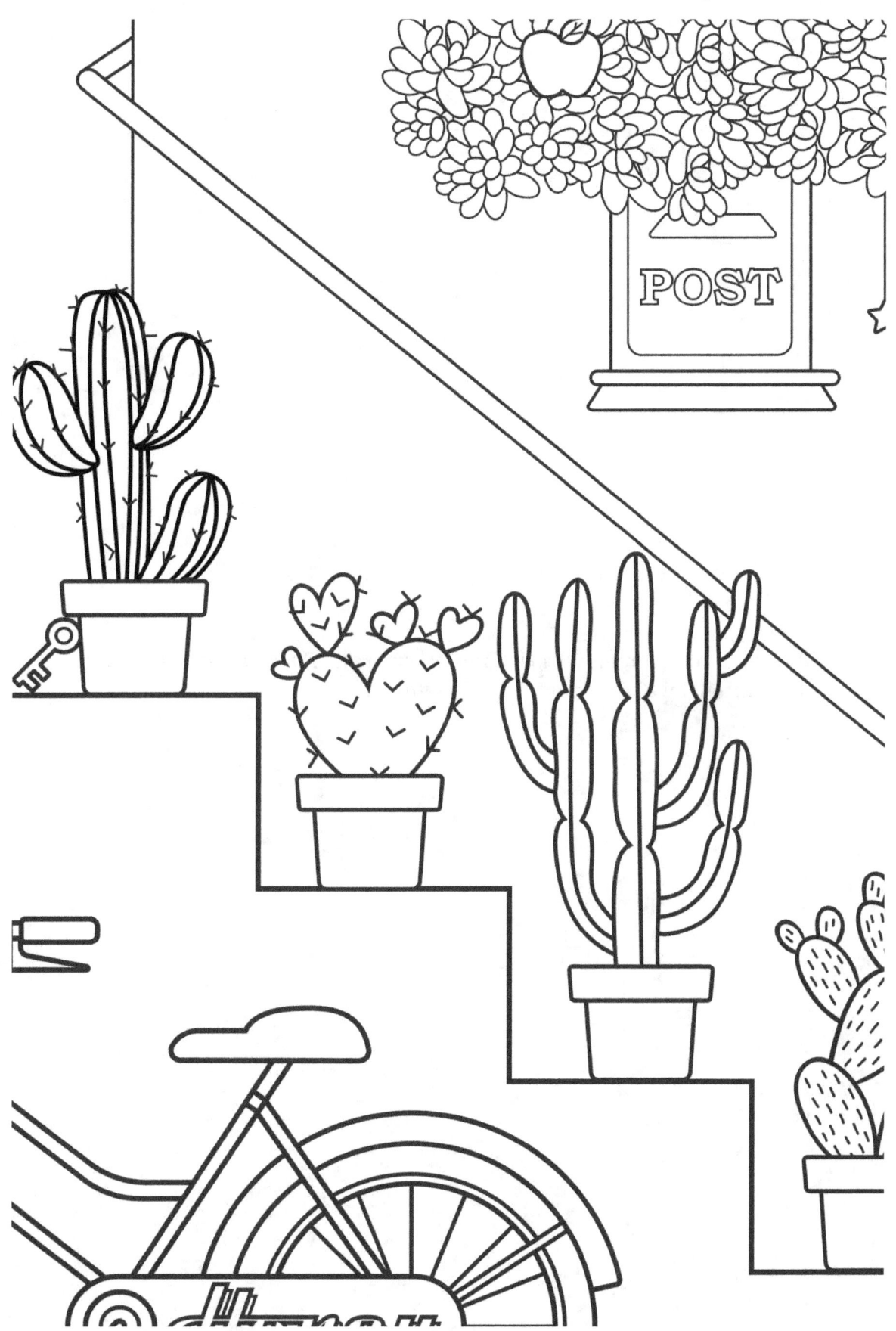

This is a Bleed Through Page. Find other great Titles by Searching for Mike Murphy on Your Favorite Book Retailer.

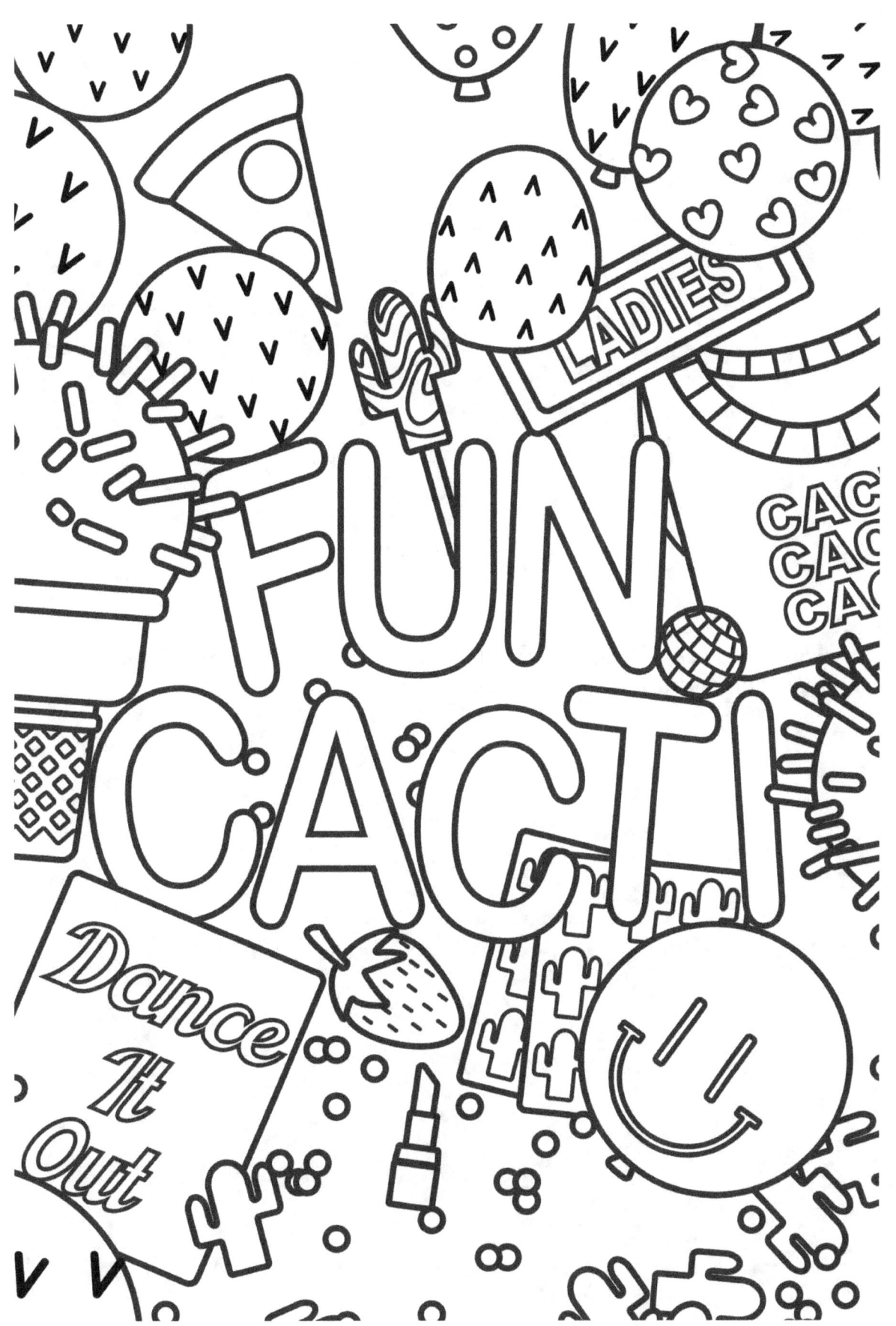

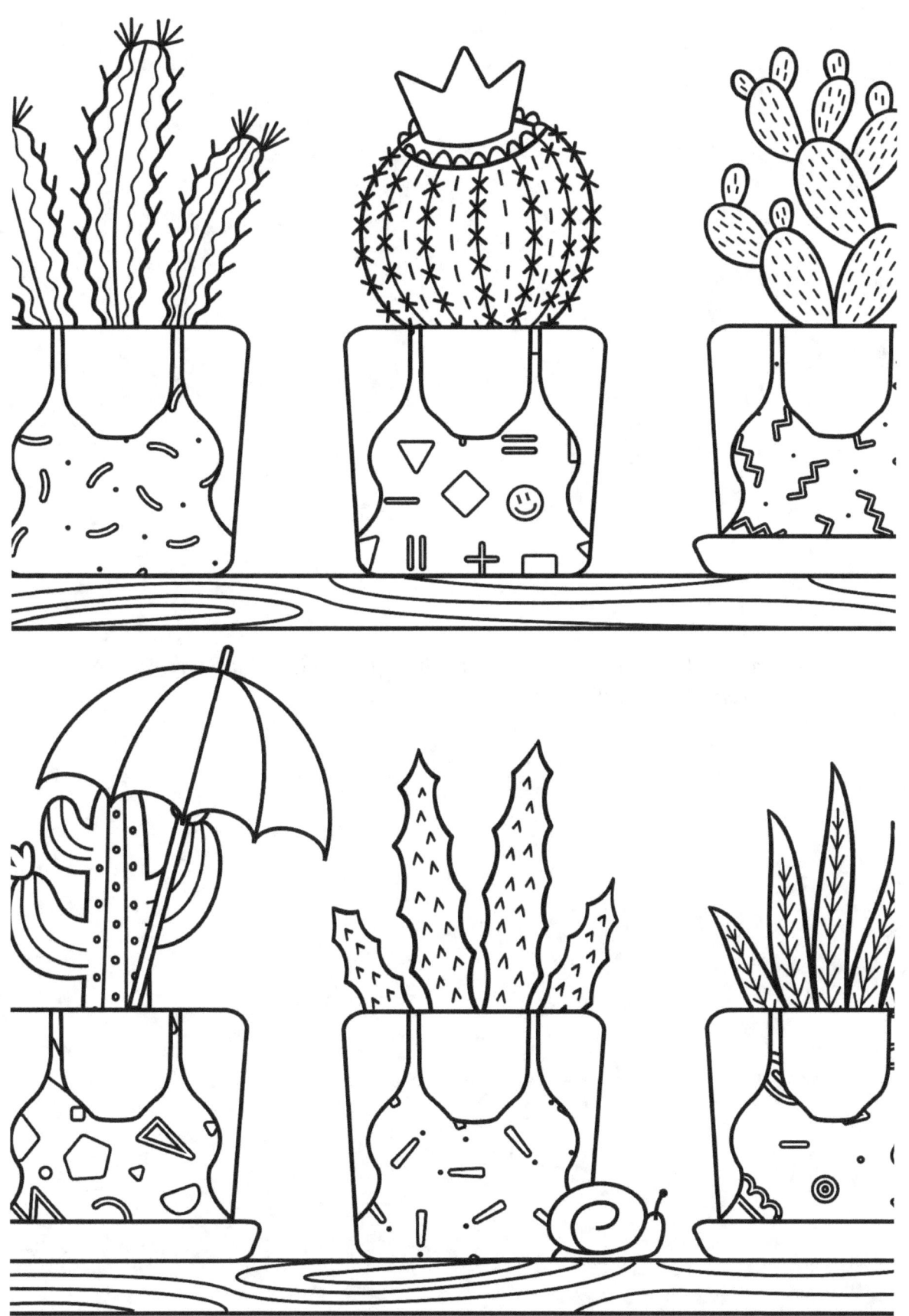

This is a Bleed Through Page. Find other great Titles by Searching for Mike Murphy on Your Favorite Book Retailer.

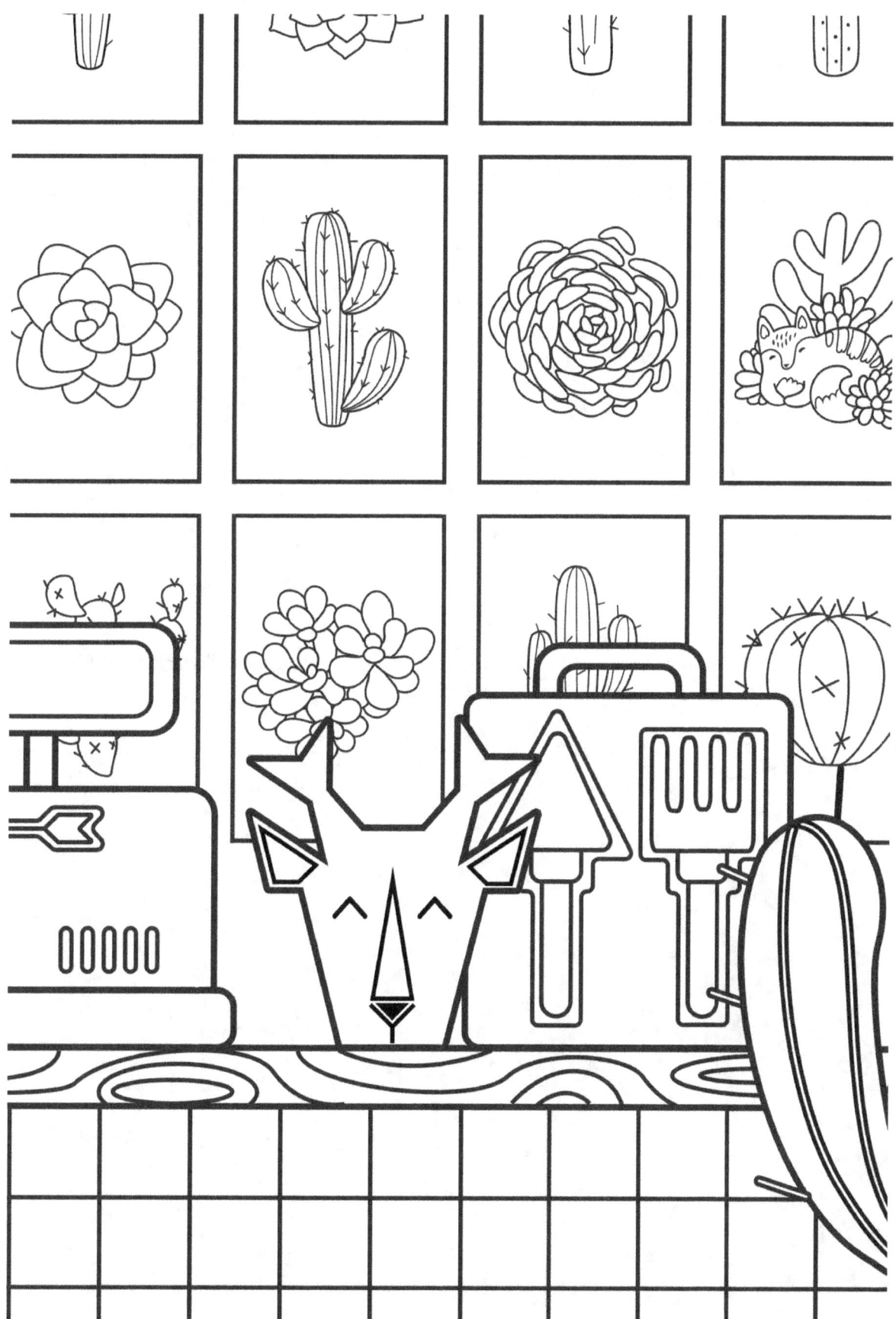

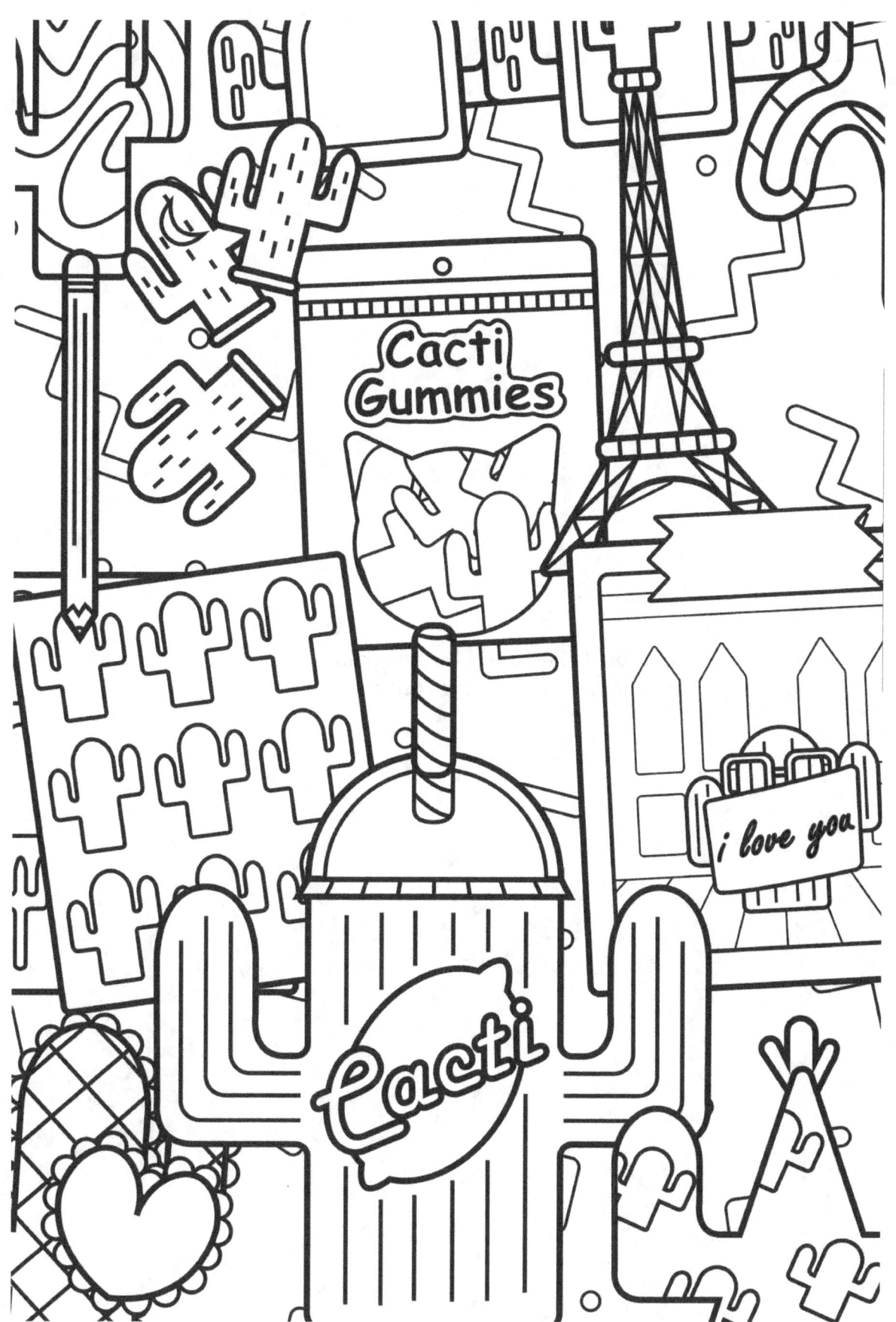

This is a Bleed Through Page. Find other great Titles by Searching for Mike Murphy on Your Favorite Book Retailer.

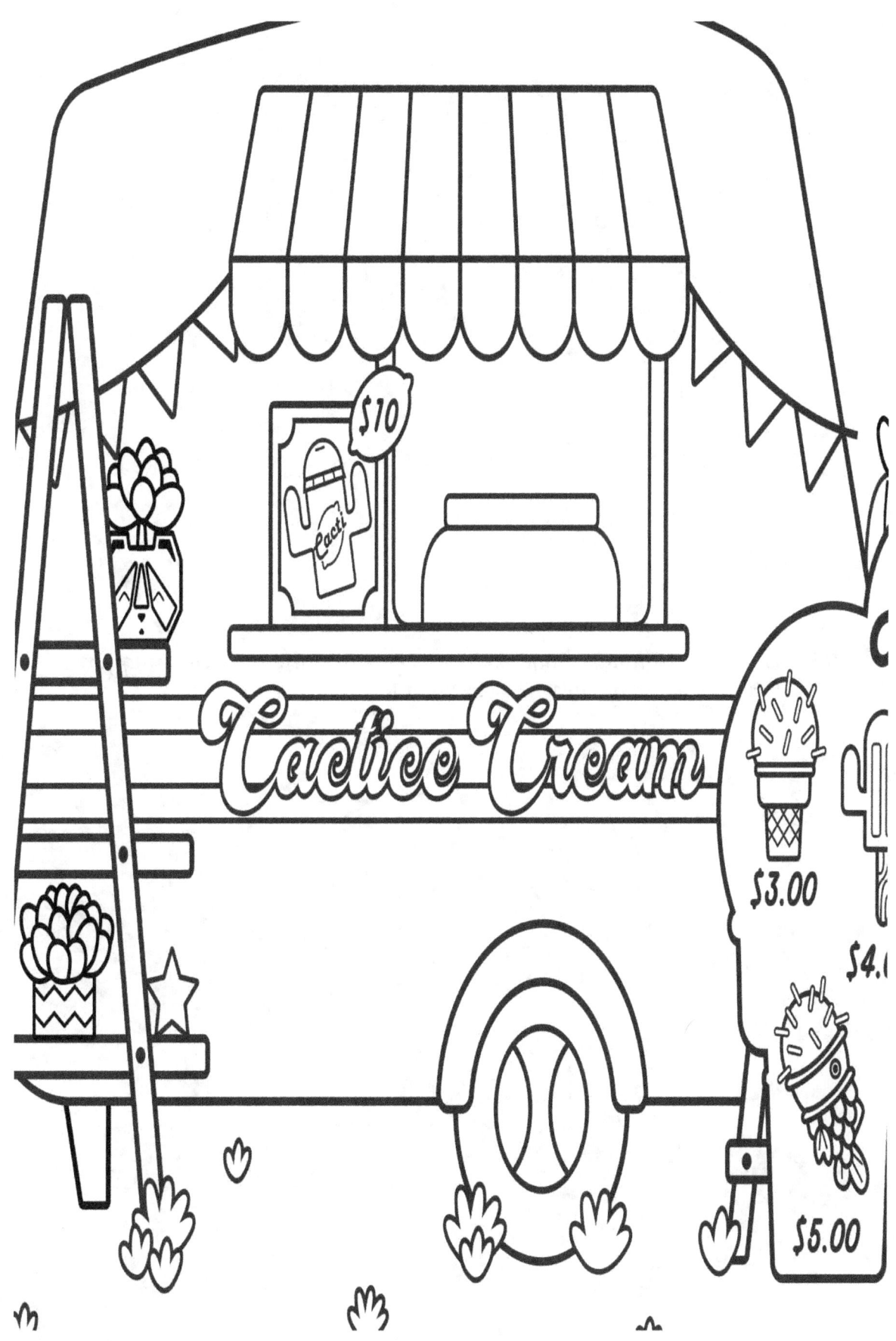

This is a Bleed Through Page. Find other great Titles by Searching for Mike Murphy on Your Favorite Book Retailer.

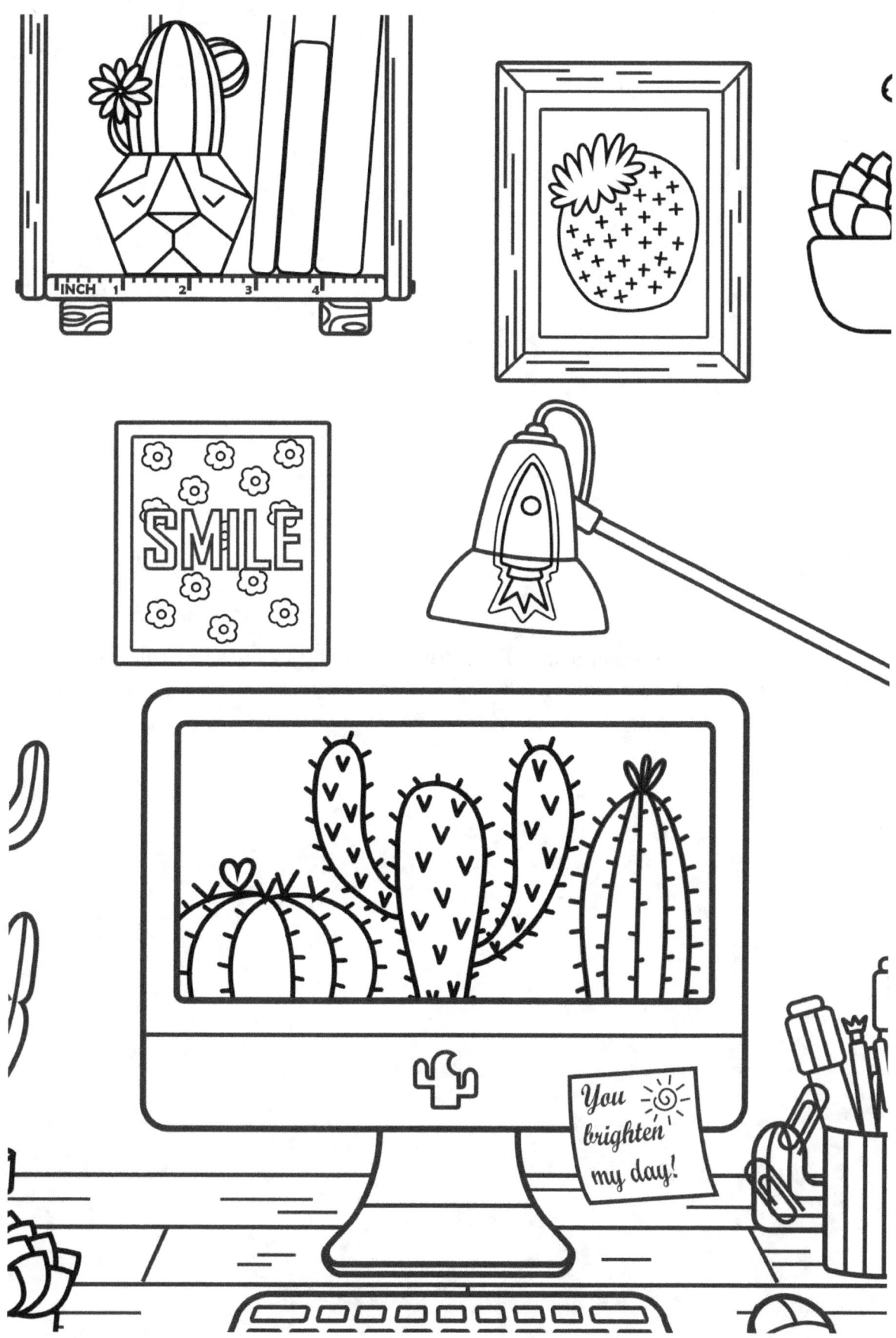

This is a Bleed Through Page. Find other great Titles by Searching for Mike Murphy on Your Favorite Book Retailer.

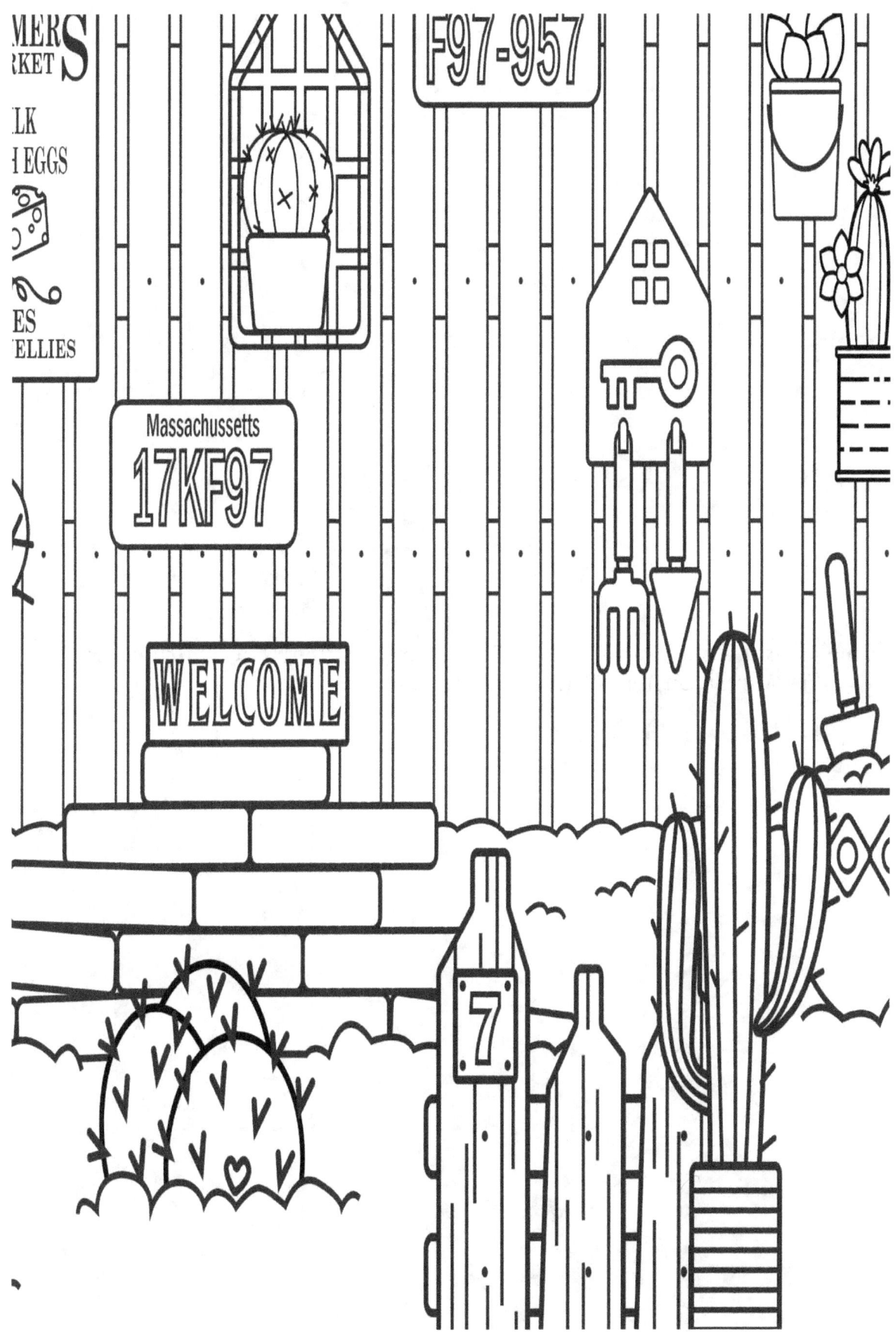

This is a Bleed Through Page. Find other great Titles by Searching for Mike Murphy on Your Favorite Book Retailer.

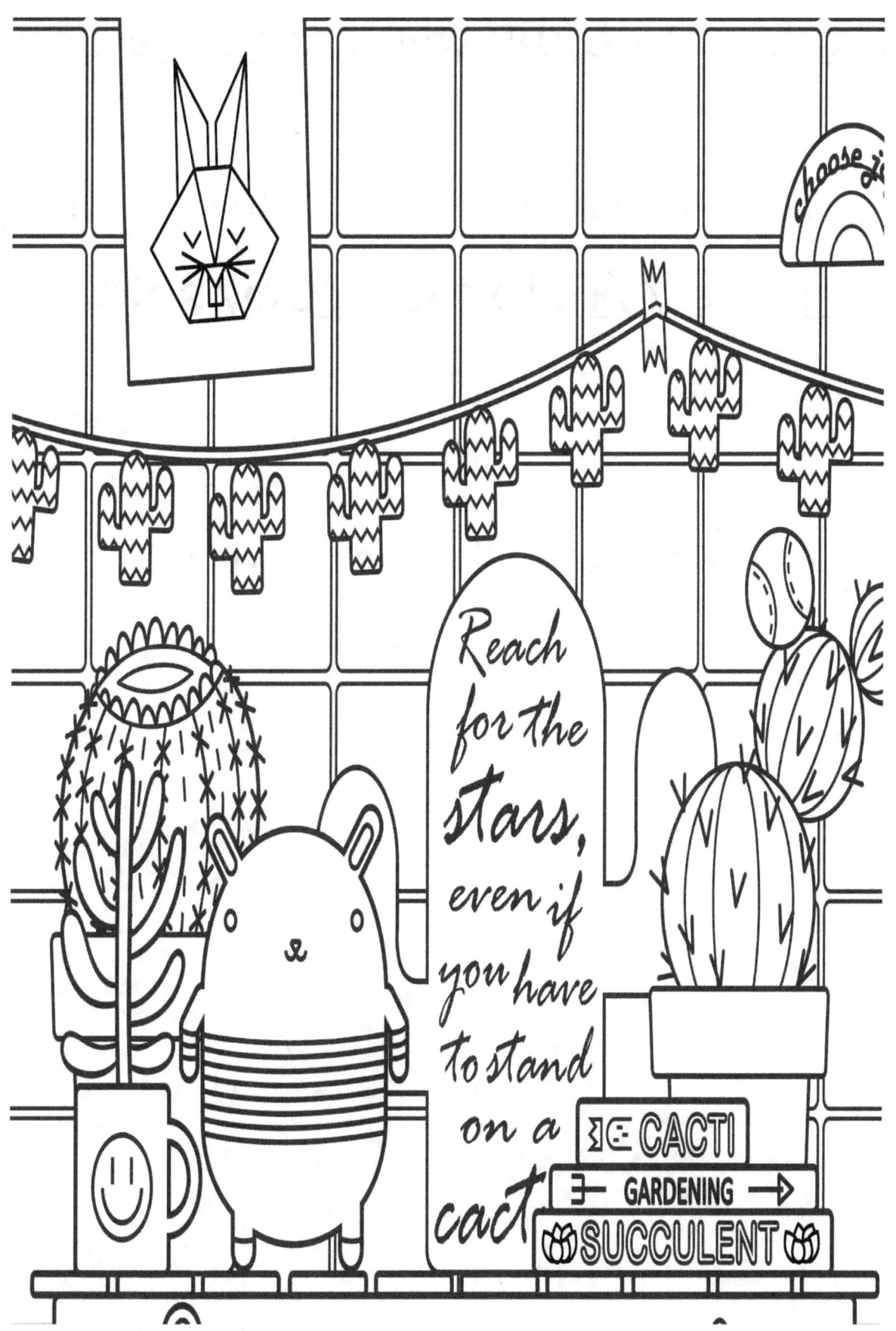

ikemurphypublish@colokara.com

Visit Below Link to Get Your Digital Version

https://colokara.com/sc2

www.ingramcontent.com/pod-product-compliance
Lightning Source LLC
Chambersburg PA
CBHW081734220526

45468CB00008B/2099